ROOM FOR Loving ROOM FOR Learning

Finding the Space You Need in Your Family Child Care Home

HAZEL OSBORN

Redleaf Press

a division of Resources for Child Caring

Illustrations by Kurt Seaberg

Published by: Redleaf Press
                  a division of Resources for Child Caring
                  450 N. Syndicate, Suite 5
                  St. Paul, MN 55104

ISBN: 0-934140-98-7

Library of Congress Cataloging-in-Publication Data

Osborn, Hazel, 1953–
     Room for loving, room for learning : finding the space you need in your family
child care home / Hazel Osborn.
          p.   cm.
     Includes bibliographical references.
     ISBN 0-934140-98-7
     1. Family day care—United States. 2. Day care centers—United States.
3. Interior architecture—United States. I. Title.
HV854.O83 1994
362.7'12'068—dc20
                                                                    94-2503
                                                                    CIP

Contents

Dedication

To my husband and love, Michael David Rothschild, who has tripped over a lot of toys. To my daughter Jean, my "junior partner," oldest child, and close friend. To my daughter Chelsea, who shared her home with dozens of other children. To my daughter Michaela, who shared her mom with a word processor. And to my parents, William Lee Osborn and Mary Elizabeth Martin Osborn, who taught me to see beauty and love, even in unlikely places. To you I dedicate this book.

Acknowledgments

Room for Loving, Room for Learning is the product of years of research and experience that would have been impossible without the help of many people. The most important were the children I cared for in my child care home and their families. The mentoring of Coleman Baker and Maureen Garber was also crucial to the success of this project. Jim Greenman provided many suggestions and resources that have been immeasurably helpful. Kathy Modigliani was helpful in providing a perspective from which to judge child care home quality.

Family child care providers Myrna Brinkmeier, Cathy Estrem, Barb Kloos, Tom and Leslie Maggi, Rita Sanft, and Ann Zettel provided many of the helpful and practical ideas in Chapter 5. They also allowed their homes to be photographed as a basis for the illustrations for this book. Eileen Nelson, my editor, provided ideas, support, resources, and assistance that were invaluable.

I wish to acknowledge and thank everyone.

Foreword

If I was providing family child care, I'd treasure this book. Because *Room For Loving, Room For Learning* is written by someone who has lived it, the book addresses the central challenge of family child care: balancing the family home and the child care home. The value of family child care lies in making full use of the family home, not confining children to a small play room. That may, however, not result in the best place to live and may put a strain on family life. Making it work for children and adults is not just a matter of love and hard work; it takes thought and creativity, and understanding the importance of a supportive environment to create a place that works for all. *Room for Loving, Room for Learning* is filled with ways to create such a place.

Children spend an enormous amount of time in child care; up to 12,000 hours. Should these be places where childhoods are spent under fluorescent lights always surrounded by children the same age? Institutional living where the individual fits the institution, standard operating procedures prevail, and most of the adult-child interactions are child management? This is not the future childhood I want for my child, or anyone else's.

Homes have some built-in advantages over center-based care in providing a "place for a childhood" and good early education, all brought out in *Room for Loving, Room for Learning.*

- Homes are human scale institutions. Serving a small number of children and families gives a day care home a head start on achieving personal relationships, flexible routes and services.

- Homes are designed and equipped for living - eating, sleeping, caring, resting, being together, and being apart.

- As important and usually misunderstood, *homes are natural learning environments* where children learn what the world is made up of and how it works, when children are engaged in the real life of the home - the cooking, cleaning, shopping. Homes are laboratories for active exploration, if you encourage the life within: the sunlight, the breezes and frost on the window. The sifting, kneading, and mixing in the kitchen. Setting the tables. Feeding the cat under the ledge and the birds outside the window. The skills for reading, writing and counting are all a natural part of the home environment, just as are interpersonal 'getting along' skills.

- A good home naturally has an environmental variety - "different places to be." This is important over the long day. Places of different size and shapes, with different feels and sounds, with different lighting and colors: under the piano or the tree out back, behind the couch, on the slippery chair, in the stairwell, on the deck.

- Homes easily allow "place to pause" when the world moves too fast, or one has to have space to get one's dignity back. Also, places to concentrate and focus on books and puzzles, and the work of early education are plentiful.

- Homes have natural multi-age grouping. Children learn from each other, probably more than they do from adults. They learn from playing, helping, and watching each other navigate life's waters. In a multi-age group, children are also more likely to be accepted as individuals, rather than as "one of the preschoolers."

Room For Loving, Room For Learning shows these strengths of family child care and how to capitalize on them by careful space design.

In addition, this book is both personal and professional. The style is almost conversational: "you need to control the space or it will control you" and readers learn what life was like for Hazel Osborn, family child care provider, and providers she knew. Yet the ideas and advice are thoroughly professional: using research and analysis to extend personal experience to help providers who provide care in a variety of circumstances.

The seamless weaving of the personal and professional in *Room for Loving, Room for Learning* captures the essential value of family child care. At its best, family child care is intensely personal - relationships based on affection and trust and individual responses to human conditions in a setting that reflects a personal way of life.

In the end, the environment works for us or against us as we try and accomplish our goals. Hazel Osborn has given us a book that helps the environment work for all the children and adults who spend their time in family day care homes.

Jim Greenman
Author of *Caring Spaces, Learning Places*
Early Childhood Consultant

Introduction

I didn't plan it this way, but my entire life has revolved around children. Like many child caregivers, I was the oldest in a large family (six children) and spent many hours helping my mother care for my younger brothers and sisters. I had been away from home only a few short months when my oldest daughter, Jean, was born.

The mid-1970s, when Jean was a baby, were the dark ages of child care; good care was scarce. By the time my daughter started elementary school, I had decided to open a family child care business so that I could be home for her after school. I planned to provide child care for only a few years, until Jean was old enough to stay home alone. I came to like it so much, however, that I began a career and spent almost ten years as a home provider before going on to other child care endeavors. In all those years of home child care, I loved the nurturing, excitement, and tumult of having six or more children spending up to ten hours a day, five days a week, in my home.

After the first few months in business, however, I resented the way the children's toys, messes, and traffic interfered with my family's life. My daughter's bedroom was raided for her prized possessions as children passed through it on their way to the bathroom. After the children left in the evening, we had to pick our way through an obstacle course of toys just to get to the couch and sit down. The traffic through our kitchen in the morning, as parents dropped off their children, made it impossible to have breakfast in peace after 6:45 a.m. My husband got so tired of introducing himself to new families that he pinned a name tag onto his bathrobe.

I learned that one of the hardest things about having a family child care home is making the home accommodate a business *and* a family. Sometimes it seemed as if the family had to sacrifice for the child care, or the children had to sacrifice for the family. Often, the person who had to sacrifice the most was me. I felt torn between meeting my family's needs and doing a good job with the children.

It was obvious that something had to change or I wouldn't be in the child care business much longer. I wished that we could move to a house that would work better for our needs, with a special place for the children and a separate entry for their parents, but that wasn't going to happen. I was stuck with a long, skinny house, one or two rooms wide, and no hall; we had to go through rooms to get to other rooms. And we lived in Vermont, so our use of outdoor space during the long winter months was limited to an hour at most each day. Yet I was determined to make my ideal of a smooth-running child care business, and a comfortable family home, work.

That was the start of my search for the perfect arrangement of space in my home. At first, I rethought and rearranged spaces by trial and error. Each time I came up with a solution to one space problem, it seemed to cause a problem somewhere else. Time and patience won out, however. We, both family and child care, not only survived but also flourished through changes in my child care families, changing schedules, new child care regulations, Jean's adolescence, the birth of two other daughters, many repairs to our old drafty Victorian house, and two extensive renovations. In those years, I rearranged my home in at least five major ways and countless minor ones to find an ideal. Then we moved to another house and I had to start all over.

With the new house, however, I was ready. I knew how to make space work the way I wanted it to. And it did work for the rest of my years in home child care. The techniques I learned through trial and error and research can help anyone achieve a better setting for family and child care. No matter what your situation, even if you are providing child care in a small mobile home or apartment, the procedures and tools in this book can help you make your home work better for you, too.

A Step-by-Step Guide to Analyzing and Improving Your Space

In Chapter 1, we'll discuss putting the needs of you, your family, the children in your child care, and other people first when you arrange and decide to use a space. I've included tips on how to make the space accommodate the people who will use it.

People continue to be the most important reason for rethinking and rearranging space. In Chapter 2, we'll look at all the different people in your business you must accommodate. That list includes the children you care for, their families, and others connected with your business. In Chapter 3, we'll make another list of people you must accommodate —your family, including guests and extended family members. In Chapter 4, we'll examine the activities these people engage in and the kinds of space they need for their activities.

Finally, in Chapter 5, we'll look at your own space; inside and out, and use the tools in Appendix 1 to find usable space for those activities. You will also find suggestions for how to implement your plan, using not only the rooms, but also the furnishings in those rooms.

Because the arrangement of your space will be determined by your needs, those of your family, and those of your child care, it will change, just as the people do. A child care home is a growing, organic space. We can't expect to set it up once and have it work indefinitely. As both children and family change, so will their needs.

Save this book and use the tools in it whenever a major change takes place, or whenever you encounter problems that could be solved through some creative space planning. Each time it will get easier.

 And now, let's get started.

Home Sweet (Crowded) Home

Is it possible to create a place where your family and your child care business coexist peacefully? Can the two ever enrich each other? The answer to these questions is an emphatic yes. You can create the ideal child care home—one that includes plenty of space for love, laughter, and harmony—and you don't have to build an addition to do it.

Your child care home starts with a new approach to your house and ends with you in charge of how the space works. You, the caregiver, must decide to be in control of the spaces in your home, even if it means using the spaces in new and different ways. You have a right and a need to control your space, in the same way you control your schedule and the behavior of the children you work with. If you don't, the space will end up controlling you, the way it did Penny, a provider I know.

Penny had a small living room area that had to accommodate both her living room and dining room furniture. She ended up with only an alcove for the children to play in. Not only did she drive herself crazy by trying to keep six active children happy in that alcove, she also was not meeting state regulations about the play space the children needed. The children's parents were unhappy with the resulting repressive atmosphere, and Penny began to lose business. Although she was a loving, capable person, she lost clients because of her management of space.

Penny had, however, a large mudroom-type entry off the kitchen. She used the room only as an entry and exit and as a storage space for power tools and gardening supplies. If she had stored those things elsewhere or installed high locked cupboards, she could have had an ideal overflow space for her restless youngsters. She could have kept a sand table there. The children could have used the area to play with large blocks. Like most of us, though, Penny saw the space only in the way it was presented to her when she moved in. If she had taken over that space and determined its fate, it wouldn't have determined hers.

Taking control of your living space and making it work for and with you is a wonderfully empowering experience. But to make your home reach its full potential—as a place in which you and yours are nurtured, embraced, and protected—step back from it. Study your home. Don't look at the physical building and grounds, but at who is inside it. The building and grounds are tools; ones that you use for the care of your family, your business, and yourself.

When you start with people, not things, in designing space, you put the priority where it belongs. Ask yourself why you are inviting these people into your home and what the benefits are.

What Are All These People Doing in My House?

There are many wonderful reasons to have a child care business in your home; probably as many reasons as there are caregivers. Most of us begin our child care careers because we want to be home for our families and share our love with the little ones who come to us for care. Both your family and the children you care for can benefit from your business.

■ With a child care business in your home, your family will develop special relationships with the families of children in your care.

In my first year of child care, Ira joined us at the tender age of six weeks. His parents worked full-time so my family and I saw a lot of him. Four years later, Ira's baby brother, Dunstin, entered the scene. By the time Dunstin took his first shaky steps, the two boys were like family members. My husband, Michael, looked forward to sharing his after-work snack of peanut butter and crackers with the two of them (they were usually the last to leave each day). To them, Michael was a hero and a special friend. And Michael found Dunstin so appealing as an infant that he decided he wanted a new little one of his own. My daughter Chelsea was born the next year. When their family moved away three years later, the parting was bittersweet for all of us. We see them every time we can and remain the best of friends.

■ If you are a parent, the learning experiences you provide for your child care will enrich your own child's growth.

■ Your family will benefit financially, not only from your income, but also from the tax advantages of a home child care business.

■ Your own children will benefit from having the extra toys and equipment around and will have a great opportunity to form special friendships.

My daughter Chelsea's best friend and bosom buddy, Heather, entered our lives as a child care client. When we moved 1,500 miles away, the two stayed as close as ever. They wrote to each other and called each other all the time. Heather's mother and I hope that they will be friends throughout their lives.

■ The children you care for in your home benefit because they will have a consistent caregiver—you. The children's parents know that the same face will greet them every morning and that they can count on the same expectations.

The closeness between caregiver and infant is fostered in family child care settings.

■ In a home child care business, children from the same families can be together in a mixed-age group. Older ones can be "big kids," helping, teaching, and nurturing the younger ones. Little ones will have attention lavished on them and, in turn, become the older ones.

■ Having a manageable number of other children to relate to makes the day easier for the children you care for in your home. They won't be as easily overwhelmed by sheer numbers as children in a day care center can be.

■ The children you care for will expand their world by knowing all the multi-aged members of your family.

As my oldest daughter, Jean, passed through her teens, she provided a constant source of fascination for the children I cared for in my home. Her clothes, makeup, school dances, and games that she and her friends played were regularly imitated and admired. She, in turn, didn't mind the hero status one bit. And when the parents needed child care at night, she often baby-sat for them, which was reassuring for the parents and a special treat for their kids. Had they not known my daughter, the children might not have encountered the teen world for years. This experience helped everyone—including parents—to be ready for that stage of development.

These special relationships don't happen as often in a child care center—they are one of the aspects of a child care home that make it unique.

Why Is it Always So Crowded and Noisy?

Family child care is a people-intensive business. It involves many people coming and going at many different times. It involves many small people going on about their busy, messy lives, and a family going on about a family life.

As you may have already discovered, many people in a small space can be hard to manage. If we have to protect our possessions from tampering, we begin to resent those who touch them. If we are constantly forced to defend our privacy, we soon resent the company of others. If we can't get what we need without interfering with someone else, patience soon runs out and stress begins.

Inadequate space, or improperly used space, makes for difficulty in relationships. You end up putting all your energy into controlling the troublesome behavior (quarreling, pushing, grabbing, "It's mine!"), instead of focusing on the positive and accomplishing good things with the children. Ideally, a family child care home should function so that family and child care enrich each other instead of competing with each other.

Following are some of the more common problems that you and other providers might have faced when planning your space. These situations and others can make a normally calm and even-tempered person want to tear her hair out.

The first conflict is traffic; meaning controlling an area that is used for an activity as well as a passageway. For example, if you're feeding your family breakfast in the area you also use as a child care entry in the morning, your kitchen probably feels like a zoo.

Another is scheduling; working around areas that are needed for two or more conflicting purposes at the same time. For example, if your six-month-old daytime baby uses your school-age child's bedroom for napping, you'll be hearing the complaints during the summer about toys being unavailable.

Storage can be another problem. Do you have items that are kept in places where they endanger, or are endangered by, children? If your trikes are stored in the garage where your husband is restoring a vintage Chevy, you have a serious safety compromise on your hands and probably a nervous mate as well.

One last problem is conflict of needs; that is, the people who use a certain space have opposing needs, which that one space cannot accommodate. Maybe your in-laws have come for their annual two-week visit. Your family room doubles as a guest room for them, which works out fine at night, but in the daytime their possessions and medicines are a constant attraction for the kids.

 I would be ready to crawl under the bed and hide when my in-laws came to visit. And when Michael's sweet eighty-year-old grandmother spent a week with us one summer, the holdup in bathroom traffic put us back two weeks in toilet training.

Chances are good that you have (or will) encounter problems like these during your time as a caregiver. Short-term problems can seem easy to "wait out": the in-laws will go home, the baby will get older, the automotive projects will be finished. But sooner or later it will happen all over again. And each time it will take a toll on your patience and the quality of your work.

Long-term problems are those that are constant: a noisy four year old practicing her aerobics constantly interrupts your quiet, shy child who wants to paint in peace; older kids, trying to get from one place to another, knock over your unsteady toddler; the annoyance of parents as they sift through the pile of soggy snowsuits in winter or damp bathing suits in summer, looking for the one they need to take home.

Amazingly enough, the way you use your space can minimize these problems.

Making Things Better

The first step in improving your space is to assess how it is working for you, your family, and the children in your care. I have found that children who spend their time in inadequate space will soon show signs of difficult behaviors. (An inadequate space is like an inadequate diet—sooner or later the effects will show up, even though you might not hear complaints about it every day.) Assessing your space is an important step in making improvements. Even an informal assessment will help you know where to focus your energies and plans.

To evaluate your need to change your space, ask yourself how you spend your time with the children and your family. Is your time spent controlling, or is it spent in constructive, pleasant activities? Does your schedule flow easily and naturally? Or are you often herding children and family from one space and occupation to another? If you don't like the answers to these questions, take a look at your space.

To help you determine the quality of your child care home, use a wonderful tool available to family child care providers: *The Family Day Care Rating Scale,* developed by Thelma Harms and Richard Clifford. This book is available through most training resource centers for child care, or you can order it from Teachers College Press (specify the home version). This assessment tool can also help you evaluate how well you provide a healthy, nurturing child care space.

Other assessment tools available include the *Child Development Associate Credential*, the *National Association for Family Child Care Accreditation*, and the *Dallas Family Day Care Home Observation Instrument*. These tools and others are summarized and compared in a report titled "Assessing the Quality of Family Child Care: A Comparison of Five Instruments" by Kathy Modigliani of Wheelock College.

Modigliani suggests that family child care providers avoid feeling that the perfect child care home should look like a scaled-down preschool. Although some providers prefer that approach, others choose a more informal, home-focused design. Either can be great. A preschool type arrangement, with enrichment materials on display, can free you up to spend more time interacting with children informally. A home-based type arrangement encourages caregiver-planned fun activities. The important thing is to develop what feels good to you.

As stated earlier, put people (including you) and their needs first when you arrange and decide to use a space. Make the space work to accommodate the people who will use it. Control the space, don't let it control you.

Remember, your lifestyle and work style should not be dictated by the ideas of the person who built your house. The idea of designing a home around people and their needs is not a new one, but it is not a common one. The renowned architect Frank Lloyd Wright was a pioneer in this method of home design. And this method was widely used after World War II, when the homecoming soldiers and their brides began the country's biggest housing boom. But the needs of families have changed since those times. And your special needs require careful and thoughtful consideration.

Your Child Care Constellation

Each child in your child care business is unique and ever changing. Each brings a family to your home. Your business brings a host of other people, including prospective families, licensers, food program inspectors, and fire marshals. All of these people are the stars in your child care constellation. The names may change, but all relate to one another as a dynamic whole.

Most child care providers are people-oriented. They think of people as more important than possessions or institutions. As a result, it will probably feel natural to plan an environment around people's needs. But it's worthwhile to spend a few minutes thinking about why planning a space around people is the best way to do things—if only to reinforce what our instincts already tell us.

What do all the people in your child care constellation need? How can you know what they need?

Many providers have a deep intuitive sense of what others need. But being sure about others' needs means checking it out—observe these other people, talk to them, and think about them. Be a detective and look for clues that may tell you what is not obvious.

To help you get started, we'll list the needs of the stars in your constellation. Along with that list, I'll offer a method for meeting those needs: establishing activity areas. Many of you are familiar with that term from curriculum or child care training, but I am expanding the use of it as a planning tool for all the needs of your child care business. First I will explain what we mean by activity area, then move to people's needs and how activity areas can provide for those needs.

What Is an Activity Area?

An activity area is a place for something to happen. If you want a certain activity to happen (for example, playing with blocks), you have to make room or create the space. A block play area would include a flat surface for building on and an adjacent storage space for the blocks. For our use, *activity area* doesn't just refer to a learning or play area, but instead refers to all the physical spaces you will create to meet the needs of your business.

Another good example of an activity area is a dish washing area (which includes your kitchen sink, dishwasher and drying rack, storage areas for your dishtowels and soap, and the place where you stand to wash the dishes). As you might have guessed, nearly all rooms in your home have several activity areas. Your kitchen has meal preparation, food storage, dish washing, and, likely, dining areas.

When planning which activities will share a space, keep in mind the activities' compatibility—you wouldn't want a noisy block play area next to your office area where the telephone is. Nor would you create a reading activity area in an entry area where people are coming and going constantly.

An after-school quiet play activity area for older children. The area includes games, books, musical instruments, and television, all close to comfortable seating.

Some activity areas are permanent; others are temporary. You can create a temporary water play area in your kitchen. Include a water basin or water table placed on the floor with towels underneath to absorb splashes. Encourage the children to pour, stir, and wash to their hearts' content. The kitchen sink itself is another place for a temporary water play area. That activity area shares space with another activity area (dish washing), but because the two activities aren't happening at the same time, you have made room for both using only one space.

The way your rooms and the objects in them are arranged determine where each activity area is. That's why it's important to place things in such a way that one activity doesn't interfere with another. For instance, you wouldn't plan to use the same surface for meal preparation and dining, because the two activities would interfere with each other—by the time you cleared enough space for the table settings, the meal you prepared would be cold. You can use the same reasoning in planning the other activity areas in your home.

Take a peek at the sample home floor plans at the end of Chapter 4 for a visual idea of what activity areas look like.

Children in Your Child Care Constellation

In our business, children come first. Our children can range from a helpless (but probably noisy) newborn to a lanky, moody pre-adolescent. Although most child care homes have a two- to ten-year spread in children's ages, those children all have certain needs you'll have to meet in every space.

The children we care for have much to cope with. Just growing up today is hard work. We want children to thrive and reach their full potential. We can help by designing their environment to meet their needs. For example, a child should not have to balance on the edge of a counter to reach the soap when she washes her hands, or run around pet droppings as she plays outside. Nor should she have to resist the temptation to finger enticing knickknacks; instead, breakables should be out of sight and age-appropriate manipulatives should be provided for her developmental needs. If her environment is planned to avoid these problems, her energy can be spent on growing and exploring.

As needs change with age, the activity areas for children will often reflect the age of the child. There are times when you'll need separate spaces for different ages of children; for example, you won't have a colicky newborn napping with your toddlers. Or you might need two dramatic play, or make-believe, areas—one for younger toddlers and another with more elaborate equipment for pre-kindergarteners. But children also benefit from contact with those older and younger than themselves, so don't isolate them from each other.

Following is a list of nine common needs of the children in your child care constellation. These are the needs to keep in mind as you plan child care activity areas. As you read through the list, keep a pencil and paper handy. Think about the children you have and make a note if you'll need more than one area to accommodate these needs. Add your own lists of needs based on your experience.

1. Safety and Protection

Safety is our number one concern. It's the most important consideration when planning activity areas. A home can be full of dangerous items and situations. Protecting children from each other and from untrustworthy adults is important, too. Take the time to rid your home of obvious dangers. If a child is ever injured at your home, you will know that you did everything you could to prevent it.

 One day, as my husband was cleaning up from a sanding project in our greenhouse/entry, he unplugged the sander from its extension cord without unplugging the extension cord from its socket. Within seconds, one-year-old Troy, who was teething, had the free end of the cord in hand, headed right for his mouth. I snatched it from him, and he narrowly avoided electrocution or serious burns. We decided to do power tool projects somewhere else from then on.

In this kitchen, medicines are handy on a shelf over the sink, yet out of reach of children. Knives are stored at the back of the counter, which is harder for children to reach than if they were left in a drawer.

2. Healthy Surroundings

To help children learn the importance of hand washing, read *Those Mean Nasty Dirty Downright Disgusting but. . .INVISIBLE Germs* by Judith Rice (Redleaf Press, 1989). I wish I'd had that book for our giardiasis (intestinal parasite) bout. Like many communicable diseases, it made the rounds of about half the children before we finally got rid of it. Because a child care provider constantly faces the threat of disease, set up your space to minimize germ transmission.

3. Nourishment

Between infant feedings; after-school snacks; treats supplied by the children's families; and regular breakfast, lunches, and dinners, your kitchen is a busy place. All children need good food served in calm surroundings on a regular schedule.

Have separate spaces for young infants; they eat all day, and not always on schedule. Their eating space should be free from the other children's germs. An infant eating area can be small (like an infant chair on the floor in a protected corner or an infant chair that attaches to your dining table), but be extra conscious of safety. Older infants and toddlers eat four to six meals per day; preschoolers will be hungry less often but feel left out if you don't offer them food when younger children are eating. If you have both age groups, consider separate eating areas for them.

This toddler-sized table tucked under a counter provides an alternate snack space for little ones; it also serves as an art area.

Kindergarteners in afternoon session at school may need an early lunch (if you can microwave an extra lunch from the day before, you'll save time. Don't expect them to have much appetite, however; they are usually too excited about school. Their hungriest time is after school.)

Set up a few meal areas, but don't have too many; children also need a routine. Outdoor eating is fun for picnics, snacks, and messy foods like ice cream, so include an outdoor eating area in your child care space. If you have more than one meal area, you will also have some scheduling flexibility.

I used to feed my daughter Chelsea early, in a private little corner, and put her to bed when she was cranky and overtired. That made lunchtime easier for the other children and for me.

Storage is important. Try storing the children's food in special areas of the refrigerator and pantry. That will keep your family out of the food you plan to serve the children, and will let you know at a glance what you have available.

4. Rest

Every child, no matter what age, needs a place to relax every now and then. For most children under five, a regular nap or rest period in the afternoon is a regular part of their schedule. Allow space for the child who occasionally needs an extra nap, or who doesn't feel well and needs to lie down until mom or dad can pick him up.

As a rule, infants do best with private sleep spaces, and they should be able to use their sleep space anytime. Toddlers can sometimes sleep together. Though they might wake each other up, they feel comforted by the presence of other children. Seeing others sleep can exert some peer pressure on a restless toddler.

Preschoolers are more likely than toddlers to rouse each other simply because they may not need as much rest. They should have the option of taking a quiet toy or book to bed to help them relax, and they should not be forced to stay in bed more than 20 to 30 minutes if they do not fall asleep. Plan for a space the children can move to if they haven't fallen asleep after a short period of time. That space should offer quiet activities (such as looking at books or listening to soft music or a story tape) so that children still get enough rest. A quiet story, soft music, and back rubs can help the children relax enough to sleep.

School-age children need a different kind of rest. They need a little break after school when they can relax and put their feet up, maybe even nod off. Occasionally, they will need a deep sleep, especially during the first few months of kindergarten. Think about a separate area that can be commandeered part-time for this purpose. A sleeping bag or pillows tucked into a corner will serve nicely.

If you serve second shift workers or if children will nap at times when the family is home, plan for rest areas carefully.

5. Toileting

Children who are learning good bowel habits, and children who are too young to begin toilet learning, all have great need of a well-organized, easy-to-use toileting area. A clean toileting area is crucial to their health and to their comfort and sense of well-being.

Carefully plan toileting areas to allow for safety, cleanliness, and privacy. Be sure your bathroom is accident-proof, with no slippery rugs or glass containers. Make sure medications are out of reach and that the room has a door that cannot be locked by a child. The bathroom should be accessible to all toilet-trained children at all times, and it should be easy to see so that you can supervise it. It's wise to allow only one child at a time to use the bathroom. In your diapering area, have supplies and running water within reach so you don't have to leave a child you're diapering on a high surface while you get something.

This simple diaper-changing area includes the basics: changing pad (used on the floor so there is no danger of falls), diaper pail, wipes, water, and soap. Disinfectant is stored over the sink in the medicine cabinet.

6. Cuddling and Affection

Even fledgling Teenage Mutant Ninja Turtles need a cuddle every day. It's easy to overlook the need for the long snuggle or extended hug if you are busy, or if the only good cuddle space is on a couch occupied by a small army of Barbie dolls and accessories. Cuddling is a legitimate need, and should be given priority in your home—indoors and outdoors.

Create cuddling space for all ages (like a rocking chair or upholstered couch for older children); and make it a space that you can use with them or that they can use with each other.

7. Privacy

Children need privacy just as much as adults do. They have a right to be able to get away from others who are bothering them, and to avoid unwelcome prying and spying. But you still need to be able to assure their safety and keep a cautious eye on them.

Toddlers enjoy private corners where they can explore without interruption.

Privacy areas should be available at the child's option and should not be confused with a "time out" that you impose (isolation time for cooling off). Encourage children to respect each other's needs for time alone.

Infants and toddlers should have an easy way to get to a privacy area; preschoolers might prefer a less accessible one that younger children can't invade. School-age children need time alone more than others because they spend most of their days in groups. Once again, their private space should be a little hard to get to, to cut down on littler ones following them.

A card table slipcover forms this hideaway; window flaps close with hook and pile fasteners.

Be sure to allow for time alone for more than one child at a time. And don't make the mistake of using the same area for cuddling and time alone—the purpose of time alone is the opposite of cuddling.

8. Personal space and storage

Children use possessions as a way of becoming independent and as a way of expressing their identity. They should be able to bring things from home to help with issues of trust and security (for example, clutch onto Teddy or Bunny anytime they need comforting) and to play with special, important toys. We all need to know that our treasured possessions are safe, and that we can get to them. Your children must be able to get to their things and know that others will leave their things alone. Many caregivers use cubbyholes in the entryway near coat hooks for storing these items. This makes pickup and drop-off easier for parents (no frantic searches for "loveys" at 5:45 p.m.).

9. Something fun to do

Children have the need to learn about their world through play. Good quality play is the child's journey to adulthood.

Children will spend most of their time in activities that are both fun and educational. Even the tiniest baby needs to feel he has some control over what he may do. Although you must give them some limits, children ought to have as many choices as they can handle. For example, by age three, they should be able to stop playing with one game, pick it up, put it away, and choose another activity without asking permission, or needing your help. This also teaches responsibility.

There are a minimum of six types of activities you should plan areas for: large muscle development, small muscle development, language development, creative development, exploration, and sensory experiences.

■ Large muscle development (for example, climbing, swinging, cycling, crawling, running, jumping, tumbling)

Plan a gym area for young infants that is separate not only from toddlers and big kids but also from older infants. Young infants are vulnerable and need the security of a space where they will not be stepped on or crawled over. A rug on a draft-free floor surrounded by soft low furniture is better than a playpen because it is not as confining and is more flexible. If your floor is wood or tile, cover a piece of rug padding with a washable blanket for infants (the pad will keep the blanket from sliding). Include things that will encourage muscle development, like mirrors the babies can see if they lift their head, or mobiles to reach for. Remember that, in general, infant activity areas can be small—sometimes, large spaces can appear scary.

For a real thrill with a very young baby, I tied a metallic helium balloon to her ankle. The reflections as the balloon jerked were fascinating, and the more she kicked, the more it moved. Using a balloon must be carefully supervised so that the baby doesn't grab the string and wind it around herself.

Some cushions to crawl over or around and brightly colored toys with a variety of textures are good, too. For older infants this can be a little more complex, with things to pull themselves up on and things to push.

This cleverly designed unit offers gym play above, with tumbling mat and slide; cuddling space is below on beanbag chairs. Manipulative-type toys and small mirrors on the front of the unit make this activity area extra versatile.

Outside, toddlers love to climb and swing. Motion fascinates them, so a rocking horse is a favorite. Preschoolers are ready for riding toys and more complex climbers. School-age children can handle bikes, skates, and jump ropes. Have something for them to climb on, too, or they will use the trees, and not just when you are watching.

Remember to create gym areas inside as well as out for all children. Providers often overlook inside gym areas because they assume they can take the children outside. Take your cue from the children as to what large-muscle activities can happen indoors. Do they enjoy dancing? Follow-the-leader? Temporary obstacle courses? Tumbling on mats or leap frog? Games like "London Bridge" and "Ring-Around-the-Rosy" are traditional favorites, too. Plan ahead so on the days when you can't go outside, you'll have an indoor space ready for your active children.

- ■ **Small muscle development (for example, building, coloring, sewing, and typing)**

Manipulatives include puzzles, beads, small blocks, small figures, and other small toys. Manipulative areas for babies could be in the same area as the infant gym area, but babies can get tired of the same space. Place a toy-supplied tray in front of them to provide a change of scene and let the babies watch the other children, which they find fascinating. Toys that make noise and have different textures are favorites.

Toddlers are ready for more complicated toys, like blocks that link together. The blocks should be large enough to avoid choking and easy to grab and manipulate. Separate the blocks and other manipulatives for toddlers from preschoolers' toys so that each group can build without interference from the other. A large tray with small blocks, which can be stored out of harm's way between sessions, cuts down on demolition problems.

- ■ **Language development (for example, talking, stories in books and on tapes, and dramatic play or make-believe)**

Your book area (or book nook) should be located in a peaceful spot, perhaps near cuddle or privacy areas. Young children enjoy "reading" to each other and themselves as well as hearing stories from you, so they'll need regular access to the book nook. Have sturdy books for infants and toddlers, with colorful pictures of familiar objects. Store them low on a shelf.

You could even store the books on a book display rack. To make a display rack, you'll need strips of wood trim, elastic strips, nails, and a hammer.

On a wall or on the back of a shelf unit or piece of furniture, nail the wood trim horizontally about twelve inches apart, forming narrow shelves. Five inches above each piece of trim, measure an elastic strip that runs the length of the shelf (the elastic will keep the books from falling down). Nail the elastic at intervals so that each book has its own seat belt. Storing books this way lets the children see the colorful covers, and books are easier to put away and take out. If you have too many books to fit on the display rack, rotate them. That will also keep the children interested in the book nook.

Use higher shelves for older children's books, to keep the little ones from tearing the pages. When you are selecting books for older children, keep their interests in mind and have a wide variety of books available. Check your local library for books; many have special lending policies for child care facilities.

Language development happens through reading to a point, but the most important part of language development is speech. Include toy telephones, walkie-talkies, and microphones in your dramatic play (make-believe) area. The most important way to encourage language development, however, is to talk *with*, not to, the children.

Children find spaces like this one appealing. This quiet corner includes a child-sized comfortable rocker and many interesting books.

You'll need make-believe areas for any children over sixteen months. Don't fall into the trap, though, of having only a housekeeping space. An area that has a variety of props to play different games (such as, office, restaurant, hospital, or fire station) is much more interesting to children. Include versatile furniture (a table that can be a kitchen table, desk, examining table, or store counter) and props to complete the scenario. Many businesses—and parents, too—have good materials to add to your collections, free. Fast-food restaurants, for example, may give you paper hats, straws, food containers, and menus for a fast-food scenario. Organize and sort the different kinds of props in large boxes and rotate the materials so the children stay interested.

One smart provider I know has a Valentine prop box filled with heart-shaped candy boxes, artificial flowers, lace, and toy money and purses. Near Valentine's Day, she sets up a Valentine shop and the children buy gifts from and for each other. The only furniture required is a table and chairs for the storefront.

■ Creative development (for example, music, art, dancing, and movement activities)

The visual arts include painting, drawing, sculpting, coloring, and other creative activities that result in an art object. Even if you serve a wide range of ages, you don't need separate areas for older and younger children's art. Use a table (for example, a kitchen table) and have younger children sit in high chairs or on stools to use the materials. That will prevent them from being able to reach the older children's projects. Even very young children should have access to art materials for a large part of the day. Cover the art table with a sheet of paper and let them color all over it.

Don't make the mistake, however, of confusing art with crafts. All the children should be allowed to create in their own way, not forced to copy or imitate something an adult has made. Let them explore different materials, including glue, Styrofoam peanuts, foil, dry pasta, sawdust, and anything else that is safe for them. Occasionally, plan a crafts project, such as making May baskets, but encourage the children to use their creativity in decorating the object. This helps their self-esteem and confidence.

An outdoor art area is important, too. That's the place for noisier creative activities, such as woodworking. Messy art materials work well outdoors, also.

Create a music area next to your gym area because children naturally dance when they hear music. Musical instruments are best kept near the gym area because the noise they create will not interfere with the gym area activities. Have a tape player with headphones available for the child who want to listen to a tape without distraction. That can be kept in your privacy or cuddle areas.

Children of all ages enjoy music. Keep a tape player and a supply of tapes with soft music and lullabies near your infant gym area. Toys that make a noise, like rattles, are really infant musical instruments. Toddlers enjoy nursery rhyme tapes and rhythm instruments. Preschoolers are ready for playing music together, and an array of rhythm and wind instruments appeal to them. (Be sure to get in the habit of wiping off the mouthpieces with rubbing alcohol before passing them on to other children.) Schoolagers usually develop a taste for G-rated rock and roll as well as traditional children's music. They love selecting and playing the tapes themselves. They also enjoy plunking out a tune on a guitar or piano, if you have one.

■ Exploration (science and nature)

Your science area is really an opportunity for infant and toddler exploration of natural objects. For preschoolers and school-age children, science means experiencing and experimenting with nature. Having access to nature, outside, is an important part of their experience, but that alone is not enough. Create a place inside where the children can handle, take apart, measure, and categorize natural objects. Ask the children to compare objects and explore their many properties. Use containers to hold natural objects (like stones, sea shells, tree bark, birds' nests, and pine cones) and encourage the children to play with them. Rotate what's available so they will look forward to learning about new things.

■ Sensory experiences (for example, water and sand play)

Sensory play refers to handling and manipulating sand, water, shaving cream, food, or other materials that do not have their own forms. In your sensory activity areas, include a shallow pan or tray for infants to play in water or lotion that they can rub on themselves. Food is a good sensory experience for them, although it can be messy. But you'll have messes anyway, and letting them explore their food will teach them to self-feed earlier. Food play should begin as soon as solids are introduced and the child can reach and grasp. For older infants, toddlers, preschoolers, and schoolagers, direct sensory play to include shaving cream, fingerpaint, playdough, and water/sand activities.

Your sensory areas should be available all of the time because of the calming effects of those areas. Children have trouble expressing themselves because of their limited language skills. When they express themselves artistically, they often feel pressured to produce a "pretty" finished product, which can create stress. Sensory play lets them be expressive without having to speak or produce something worthwhile. Child therapists use sensory play to help troubled children work out their difficulties. If you have a child that is difficult you may find that sensory play helps to ease his or her tensions, too.

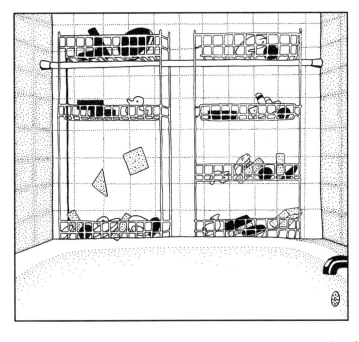

A spring-type shower curtain rod holds wire shelving for water toys along the back wall of this tub.

Some providers use rice, dry oats, or even ground coffee for sensory play. This can work, but keep an eye out for mold and insects, rodents, and other creatures that may be attracted to these materials.

Many resources are available to help you with ideas on creating activity areas. Take advantage of them. Your local resource and referral agency or licenser will be able to direct you to good sources.

A Short History of Children's Activities and Learning

In colonial times, educators thought of learning in terms of what children would need to know as adults. Teachers trained their students as if they were already adults. Children were expected to sit quietly for hours in church, learning about morality. Later, educators realized that children were different from adults, and that they learned differently, too. Jean Piaget and Maria Montessori were leaders in developing theories of learning for young children. Education for preschoolers outside the home was not widely practiced until the Great Depression and World War II, when large numbers of women (and mothers) began to work. The widespread use of formal planning for children's activities, however, was not seen until recently.

Planners for young children's activities used to be based on kindergarten-type programs. Now the best children's programs, many of which are home-based, plan for activities that are appropriate for the developmental stage of the child. This kind of plan is referred to as "developmentally appropriate." The activities mentioned in this chapter are all developmentally appropriate.

For more information on developmental appropriateness, read the publication, *Developmentally Appropriate Practice in Early Childhood Programs Serving Children from Birth through Age 8* by Sue Bredekamp. This book is available for a low cost from the National Association for the Education of Young Children, 1509 16th St. NW, Washington, DC, 20036-1426, 1-800 424-2460.

Well-Planned Play Areas

What's a quick way to find out if your play areas are well planned? See if the children are using them! If the children ignore or don't use an area the way you had planned, or if they don't use the toys in the area, re-evaluate your plan. Don't assume that because the children aren't using an area that they are not interested in that particular activity.

In their book *Planning Environments for Young Children: Physical Space*, Sybil Kritchevsky and Elizabeth Prescott discuss the number of play stations children need. A play station is a spot designed for one child to play in. For example, a swing set with three swings has three play stations, one swing for each of three children. But if you take down one swing and replace it with a glider, there are now four play stations, two swings, and two places on the glider. Kritchevsky and Prescott recommend that you have at least two-and-one-half play stations for each child in your care; three per child is better. If you serve six children daily, you will want at least fifteen play stations; with eighteen being an ideal number.

Kritchevsky and Prescott also discuss three different types of play units. The first is a simple unit, one that can be used in only one way. A swing is an example of a simple play unit. The second is a complex unit, which has two different types of materials and can be used in several ways. An art table with paper and crayons is a complex unit. The third type is a super unit, which has at least three types of materials and will hold children's attention the longest. A water table with funnels, spoons, and tempera powder is a super unit. Thinking of your space with these ideas in mind will help you plan activity areas that hold children's attention.

When planning activity areas, keep each separate and unique. That will remind children to keep materials in the appropriate areas. Using the same space all the time for the same activities will also give stability to their play. This enhances learning and lets them accomplish complicated tasks (energy is not being constantly used up on learning about new displays and new equipment).

Remember to plan play areas for indoors and out, with as much variation as possible. This multiplies the choices the children have and makes the most of your space.

Ordinary household items, like these quilts, transform furniture into fantasy dwellings.

A Controversial Activity: Watching Television

We could think of the television as a tool or a material like any other. But unlike most materials, the television tends to dominate because of its noise and flickering light. With this in mind, keep the television in a closed-off area. Use a portable TV for special occasions; for example, if you're having a party with a special program. Since watching TV can fulfill a variety of functions in a variety of areas, keep the TV space flexible, but apart from everything else.

Many providers aren't sure where TV watching fits in to their daily routine. If used properly, watching television programs can be educational and stimulating or relaxing and fun. But try to stay away from using the television to keep the children busy for extended periods of time. The children will not benefit from staring at the TV screen, and their parents won't appreciate it, either. Instead, use the television to complement activities. For example, rent a videotape of *Dumbo* to show the week you have a circus prop box in your make-believe play area.

As much as I hate to see children glued to the tube, there are times when watching television programs really helps. The day after Christmas is a good example of when stretching out in front of the TV seems the most one can hope for. When children are exhausted, overwrought, and overstimulated, and you need to get them through the day, a little TV helps.

If you use the TV regularly, try to make it an activity, not a "passivity." This means interacting with whoever else is watching. These interactions can include friends watching together and discussing it, you interacting with the children about what is happening, children acting out what they've seen on TV (they love to do that, so pick the programs carefully), and sharing with parents what they've seen on TV. You can use TV for special occasions, too, like a special holiday videotape.

Special Considerations When Planning Activity Areas

When planning activity areas, consider the developmental stage of each child. If you know each child's development, you will be able to identify and anticipate their needs. The chart below will get you started. Of course, there is a range of ages associated with each new skill; these are only approximations.

Developmental Stages

Age	Physical	Emotional	Social	Cognitive
6 wks.	raises head	quiets when held	cries when hungry/tired	follows with eyes
3 mos.	raises head and shoulders	prefers mom	smiles at people	recognizes people
6 mos.	sits when supported	frightened by angry voice	enjoys watching children	recognizes own name
9 mos.	has pincer grasp	upset at parent's leaving	babbles to others	"gets" some words
1 yr.	pulls up to stand	fears strangers	tries to join play	has 1 or 2 words
18 mos.	walks alone	asserts independence	makes demands	has 12-40 words
2 yrs.	runs, jumps	relies on routines	imitates others	uses short sentences
3 yrs.	can walk on a balance beam	eager to please	forms close relationships	converses easily
4 yrs.	likes to ride tricycles	boisterous, bounces ball	argues with friends	imagines "what ifs"
5 yrs.	climbs with ease	has school apprehensions	negotiates with friends	writes own name

When planning play areas, keep in mind children with special needs. These children have extra or different needs than those of the other children you serve. Children in the middle of certain parental issues, such as drug-addicted or very young parents, or children with learning or physical disabilities have special needs.

If you are serving a child with special needs, the parent and professionals who work with the child can help you plan activities to serve that child. Look for that support in order to keep yourself from burning out as a result of the extra effort you give to the child.

Attitudes and personalities of your children are two other points to keep in mind when planning your space. Think about the kind of person each child is, regardless of the stage of development. Is the child outgoing or shy? Energetic or lethargic? Contemplative or daredevil? What does each child like to do most?

To help show how children's individuality should be a part of your planning, following is a list of children. The list includes their individual concerns and activity area suggestions for them.

Name	Age	Needs
Mark	2 mos.	flexible schedule; visit from mom at noon for breast-feeding; extra time with big sister, Annette; quiet, low-noise places
Brenda	20 mos.	extra morning snack; chance to practice new words; time away from animals (has a fear of being bitten)
Carl	3 yrs.	toilet training help; same schedule each day; time to work out temper tantrums; time with Brendon
Annette	3 1/2 yrs.	patience (has a short, 5-10 minute attention span); time to work things out (is easily frustrated); time to work out feelings for new brother, Mark; work with speech (which is delayed)
Deena	4 1/2 yrs.	activity (is physically restless); people to talk to; place to play with Barbies
Brendon	5 yrs.	quiet time instead of a nap; time away from Carl; reassurances about riding school bus; place to play Superman
Lydia	7 yrs.	after-school schedule; outdoor activities; time alone when cranky and moody; place to read

Sample Activity Areas for Children

We'll discuss these areas in the home layout section in Chapter 4.

INDOORS

Transition/Entry	one or two: indoor/outdoor play; arriving/leaving
Meals	three: infant, toddler, and preschool/ school age
Rest	two: infant and toddler/preschool
Toileting	two: diapering and toilet-trained
Cuddling	two: infant/toddler and preschool/school age
Privacy	two: infant/toddler and preschool/school age; and cubbies
Gym	three: infant, toddler/preschool, and school age
Small Manipulatives	three: infant, toddler, and preschool/school age
Book Nook/ Dramatic Play	offer two options
Art/Music	three (one for each gym area)
Exploration	two: infant/toddler and preschool/school age
Sensory Play	one or two: sand, water
TV	one

OUTDOORS

Meal	one or more
Cuddling	two: infant/toddler and preschool/school age
Privacy	two: infant/toddler and preschool/school age
Gym	two: infant/toddler and preschool/school age
Small Manipulatives	three (as indoors)
Art/Music	one (near gym area)
Exploration	two: infant/toddler and preschool/school age
Sensory Play	one

Adults in Your Child Care Constellation

Even though the needs of the children are most important, remember to consider other people when planning your child care space. These people include the children's families (immediate and extended), potential clients, and colleagues (licensers, fire marshals, food program inspectors, trainers, substitutes, emergency backups, pediatricians, and other caregivers). Keep in mind the needs of support professionals, including visiting nurses, consultants or representatives of training programs, the Child Care Food Program, your local library, the National Association of Family Child Care Homes, or a local child care organization. Following is a list of five common needs these people require. Add your own list of needs based on your experience.

1. Entry and exit

Parents need to easily enter, drop off or pick up children, and exit. Of course, it's never as simple as that because good-byes and hellos can be difficult. That's why the entry and exit area is a crucial one to plan well.

This transition area is a busy one. In addition to walking in and out, children will be dressing or undressing, putting their things away or searching for toys, and saying hellos and good-byes. It's sometimes tempting to create separate exit and entrance spots for different age groups, so that older, more dexterous children can get in or out without tripping over the younger ones. But separate areas create a problem when children of different ages are from the same family and Mom or Dad drops all the possessions in the same place. For this reason, organize the space by families, as long as the children are preschool or younger. However, you might need a separate area for schoolagers. These older children may come in during naptime and need different storage for backpacks, school projects, and wet outerwear. Some might come in alone instead of with a parent.

Entry areas are complicated because, although they are fairly public with everyone coming and going, much intimate communication happens there. The long good-byes, happy greetings, and sometimes tense adult-to-adult relating can be impossible to do well with a stream of people rushing through. And if a mother needs to nurse her child before leaving, the entryway will not work. To resolve these situations, create a space for breast-feeding moms and ask a parent to move to your office area for any extended talks.

If someone is having trouble saying good-bye, tell them they can retreat to a more private space. A good technique to ease separations is to ask the parents to call you when they get to work. That way, you can reassure them that their child has stopped crying and is playing happily. Likewise, a child who is upset may benefit from a call to her parent.

This parent information center gives adult-eye-level access to schedules, menus, news, and parent education materials.

The transition area is ideal for sharing information with parents via a bulletin board. Photos, schedules, plans, menus, and information on child development and other relevant items will catch a parent's eye.

2. Parking

Good parking is important for parents' convenience, your family's accessibility, and your neighbors for minimizing intrusions.

The parking area should be safe and separate from children's play areas. To make a good impression, it should be well-lit and clean. The walkway to your home should be free of clutter and, in winter, ice-free. When parents arrive at your house, they will be carrying bags and children and might not see an obstacle. Remember that their arms will be full, so make sure your door is easy to open. A large table or counter immediately inside the door will provide a place to set their burdens down. Labeled cubbyholes, hooks, and shelves are a must. And chairs or a low bench are necessary for helping children with boots and shoes.

The parents will do most of their business with you—parking, entering, set-down, dressing or undressing the child, conferring, leaving (or greeting the child), getting feedback from you, gathering belongings, paying you, and exiting past the other parents—all in this space. Its appearance is important in maintaining a businesslike impression.

3. Special events

Picnics, celebrations, and end of year parties can help you get to know your families better and help them make friends with one another. These events, however, put a strain on your space if all the families are there at once. Plan ahead for extra parking needs and plenty of space for circulating and visiting if you are having a party or show for the families.

Some providers like to have parent meetings where parents can get to know each other, or work together on common goals, such as a support group or a field trip. As you develop professionally, you may often find yourself on committees. If the gathering is business-oriented, you'll need a meeting space, a surface to write on, and a way to serve refreshments. If the gathering is social, you'll need conversation or party space.

 My first year of child care felt like a three-ring circus. But by the end of the year I was proud of what I had accomplished with the children and wanted to show off to the parents. The children and I planned a holiday party, complete with invitations, entertainment, and refreshments. The parents loved it and enjoyed socializing. An extra benefit was the pride the children felt to be hosts. The parents decided to form an informal support network among themselves. Their network was strengthened each year at what became our annual party.

4. Observation space

This can be as simple as providing an adult-sized chair for a prospective client, special needs consultant, or licenser, but it can keep your day from being disrupted.

Consultants and licensers need a way to inspect your program without interfering too much in your routine. They will need a surface for materials and writing and easy access to your program information and records. They may also need to use your telephone.

Of course, you want to present your home at its best to prospective clients. When they visit to observe your program, provide a place for them to sit without interfering and a chance to ask questions.

 I'll never forget my first meeting with Carl's mom, Lynne. Following advice in a magazine, she dropped by unannounced, right after naptime. Unfortunately, a pot of beans had burned that day and it was a charred, smelly mess. To keep the fumes out of the house, I had put the pot on the porch. This was the first sight that greeted Lynne. Luckily, she had a great sense of humor and we had a good laugh about the first impression I had made. I seated her in a corner and she observed our snack and table toy time. She liked what she saw and Carl spent the next four years in my care.

You may also have visitors to supplement what you offer the children; perhaps you've hired a clown or magician for entertainment or asked a new mother to bring her baby for a special show and tell.

Soon after a friend gave birth, I called to ask if she would like to show off the baby to my little ones. She was more than willing, and the visit fascinated the children. It turned out to be good planning, as a few months later I presented them with a baby of my own. Many of them remembered what they'd learned about newborns.

5. Substitute space

There is one more important professional contact to plan space for: your substitute. You do have a substitute, don't you? If not, put this book down and find one.

Be sure to design space so that everything is easy for your substitute to find and use. She'll have her hands full with children and parents and shouldn't have to search for things. Provide clear directions, easy layout, and quick access to emergency phone numbers and first aid supplies.

 For years I resisted using a substitute. When I finally did, I could have kicked myself for waiting so long. Eventually, I hired Alice full-time. After nine years, I was ready for a new job, but I wanted my four year old to be in her home with the friends she had always had. And just as I was accepting a new job, I discovered that we had a baby on the way.

The solution was a partner who would operate the business while I started my new job and care for the baby after she was born. It was complicated, but Alice and I managed it so well that when my family moved a year later, she continued the business in her own home.

The Superstar of Your Constellation

This section is about you. Without you, the entire constellation would collapse. So take a few minutes to think about your needs. Following are five common ones.

1. Time

Time is your most precious asset. With so much to do and so many to care for, you don't have thirty seconds to waste. You need up-to-date equipment and appliances. If you don't have an answering machine, cordless phone, intercom, and microwave, as well as on-site laundry facilities, make them a goal for yourself; they are worth their weight in gold.

2. Good organization

You need to know where the children are and what they are doing at all times. With that in mind, set up play areas within earshot. Put phone numbers and names at your fingertips. Keep the house quiet enough for conversation and for you to hear a whisper when you need to. Keep loud activities on the periphery.

3. Preparation space

You'll need a space for preparation, storage for publicity and marketing materials, and a space for record keeping and program, meal, shopping, and activity/field trip planning. Most of these activities will probably happen in your office area, although some might happen right in the children's areas. For supervision, you need all children's areas to be easily accessible. You'll need to be able to prepare meals, clean up, and use the bathroom. You'll be diapering, cleaning, gathering materials, packing children's belongings, and greeting and conferring with parents. Most important, you'll be communicating with and relating to children. Your activity areas should help make that happen easily.

4. Office space

An office area can include conference space (a place to sit down and discuss things quietly with parents). It should be private and have room to spread out materials to share with them. You'll use this space, too, for your other business associates. There may be more than one adult meeting with you on occasion, like when you chat with both parents, or several at once in a planning session. So allow enough room for several people.

Experienced caregivers find that a separate office space, like this computer dock tucked into a closet, is ideal.

5. Storage space

You'll also need space for storing items adults leave with you, such as books, a child's medicine, or donated materials. Remember, parents have a right to inspect your program at any time; in many states that is a licensing regulation. During parent, licensing, and other visits, you will want to get to your records easily. For example, you might need a form for a parent or an immunization record to show a licenser. Having your office area include conference space and records space saves preparation time, and creates a more professional impression.

Remember that you have a right to a career—not just a job—and professional support, including a desk/planning area, organized supplies, and resources. You deserve respect for what you do from others. Your work/planning area should not be squeezed in between the stove and sink, or overrun with the family correspondence and old magazines.

Sample Business Activity Areas for Adults

We'll discuss these areas in the home layout section in Chapter 4.

Office/Meeting

Entry

Parking

Special Events (not always in use)

Observation

Your Family Constellation

In Chapter 2, you read how important it is to consider children's needs when you plan their activities and design your space. The same is true of your family. In fact, the needs of your family are greater and more complicated than the needs of the children you care for and their families. Don't forget, they live here.

It can be hard to live in a child care home because your family has given up some privacy and quiet. Of course, they also benefit from your business, but try to make things as easy as possible for them if you want your business to last.

A family that's unhappy living in a child care home will make their feelings known, not just to you, but to anyone who will listen. For example, if you ignore your son's complaining about children invading his bedroom, he may take his irritation out on the children, or their parents, in subtle ways. The overall effect on your business will be a bad one. Your family must be a partner with you in business because they share the home with children in your care. And you won't have a cooperative partner in them unless their needs are met, with space for their activities.

To a degree, you're already an expert on what the family activities are. You're home all day, and you know what's going on in the house. In addition, most families already have well-defined activity areas.

But looking at those areas again can benefit you. You may find needs that don't have space (perhaps you will suddenly realize that your child won't share his toys because he has no place to keep them separate). You may also find space your family doesn't need (maybe you've devoted a corner of your living room to a pinball machine that your college-age son doesn't use any more).

Judicious use of toys can add charm to your home as well as new play options for children.

As you think about your family's activities, ask family members for their ideas. They should be involved in planning. Keeping their wishes in mind will gain you their cooperation and enthusiasm for your business. And if they are included in your plans for change, they will be more helpful when the changes happen.

In this chapter, we will look at some general needs of families and some needs that are specific to the age and place in the family of certain family members. Then we will look at suggested activity areas that can meet these needs. Remember that the needs and activities of your family are more complicated than those of the children in your care and their families; give the planning for your family the time and attention they deserve.

Needs Shared By All

Following are six concerns for all family members, from a newborn to a great-grandfather. Some of these needs were mentioned in Chapter 2 for children in care, but a family's needs have a different emphasis. As you read this section, think about your family and make a note if you'll need more than one area to accommodate these needs. Add your own lists of needs based on your experience.

1. Safety and Protection

The family needs safety from your business. Your aging mother-in-law needs to be able to cross the living room without tripping over blocks and toys. Your infant needs protection from the curious pokes of children in care. Other family members will have similar concerns, but theirs will vary by the age of each person. A concern for all of them is the traffic at drop-off and pickup times; visibility should be good and parking should not interfere with walkways.

2. Healthy Surroundings

The primary danger to your family's health is exposure to germs and disease from the children in care. More than one adult in a caregiver's home has gone to the doctor's with a nasty sore throat, only to find the doctor diagnosing Coxsackie virus (a disease normally seen in children under five). Not only are the sanitary habits of children usually poor, but they also pass germs to each other, multiplying the chances that your family will catch them, too. Encourage hand washing to your family as much as you do to the children. Keep the house easy for them (and you) to clean, or it won't be cleaned often enough. Wastebaskets, cleaning supplies, and storage must be handy.

3. Communication

You can't limit communication to an area because interacting with others happens in many ways. Communication is a crucial part of a family's mental health. Families need private space to talk with each other, even during business hours. Make sure at least one room has no child activities and use that room if your family needs some communication time. If that is impossible, shut down an activity area from time to time for urgent conversations.

I hate to admit it, but sometimes my husband and I snapped at each other in front of the children in my care (at the end of the day, when tempers are short, it's an occupational hazard). I soon learned to say, "Let's save this for later," or "Let's take this into the next room." I also learned to reassure children who heard the tension in our voices that grown-ups sometimes get annoyed at each other, but they still love each other. I made sure they saw evidence of the love as well as the irritation, and I know this gave them a good model for how to relate to their future mates.

The phone is a tool for communication that is often in demand. Consider having more than one line (one tax-deductible phone for your business, the other for family) or call waiting service (no nagging your children to get off the phone when you're expecting a business call), and an answering machine.

4. Affection

The family may feel displaced by your business, especially when you cannot give them your attention. Let them know that they will get your attention after-hours. When a problem arises during business hours, plan a special time later on when you can help. Remind them that you have a responsibility to your work even when you might like to put it aside for a while. Meanwhile, be sure the family member has a private space away from the children in your care to deal with the problem.

5. Autonomy

It can be easy to forget that your family needs breathing space to do what they want. As you try to control what happens in your home during the day, you may fall into the drill sergeant habit, pressuring your family to stick to a certain arrangement and schedule. You might tell them not to make any new demands on the space or your time. Remember, however, what home is supposed to feel like. You will need to be at least as flexible for your family as you are for your business. A predictable routine from you lets family members make plans. They should not have to consult with you every time they want to do something; the routine and space should be consistent so that they can plan around them. Letting family members be independent can reduce the chances of stressful situations.

6. Privacy

Family members need privacy, not only from peering little eyes (children get especially curious when they sense someone is upset), but also from the children's families. Your clients do not need to know about the difficulties your children might be having with school or best friends, and they also don't need to know about the fight you and your husband had last night. (They probably don't want to know, either; you will seem less professional if you tell them.) Your family needs a place they don't have to share with your business. That space is the essence of what home is—one's own space where no one else may be, unless invited. No matter how small your home, it's big enough for each member of the family to own at least a small space. If two of your children share a bedroom, they are likely to need extra privacy. Make sure each one has at least a corner to call his or her own.

Just as you expect your family to respect your business, you must make it clear to client families that they need to respect your family. The families will be concerned (rightfully) about what sort of people their children are exposed to, but that does not give them a right to impose their values on your family. Most families make an effort to be friendly and respectful, and often a warm relationship develops between your family and theirs. But if this is not the case, set limits about intrusions.

What's Special About Each Person in the Family?

Let's look at the family, one member at a time. Your family may be small and include just you or you and a spouse, or larger including yourself, a spouse, children, adult family members, and pets. Like the children you care for, each family member needs to be considered as an individual.

The first family member we'll talk about is you. Most providers have a tendency to put themselves last, not first. But you are an important person, the one who has to make this business happen. Your needs are important, too. You may think that you're strong enough to do without; that if you sacrifice your own needs for a while, they will be met later. Unfortunately, the more you put off your needs, the less important they will seem to you or others. You will, however, experience stress and resentment as your needs are not met. The danger is that those feelings will cause you to burn out.

 When I began my child care business, I wanted to take care of small chores (making phone calls or trimming the lawn) during naptime. I overlooked the fact that I needed to refresh myself, not to work more, at naptime. After a few weeks of mounting exhaustion, I learned to use that time for relaxing.

Caring for children in your home can give you a split personality. You now have both professional and home identities. Some providers blend them seamlessly, but many feel more comfortable if the two are separate. It's important that others recognize *both* of your roles—your professional one (in the case of your family) and your family one (in the case of your clients). When the line that separates the two gets blurry, you end up trying to meet everybody else's expectations instead of your own.

As I have stated before, I strongly urge providers to get and use an answering machine. That way, you can eat dinner or watch a movie without being interrupted by parent calls. Frequently, a call is necessary only to give you information, so running to the phone every time it rings isn't a good use of your time, either.

As you think about your space, take your own personality into account. What's important to you; what makes you feel good about your day? Do you have a retreat that is all yours? Is a coffee break with your favorite mug essential to a smooth morning? (If so, you will need space to do that.) Does hunting for game pieces drive you nuts? (If so, game storage and use areas will be important.) If your circumstances are especially stressful, give yourself extra leeway. Perhaps your spouse is only seasonally employed or you are a single parent, pregnant, or have a health problem. Those circumstances might mean you need to be extra kind to yourself.

Consider your stage of life, too. Are you just striking out on your own? Social networking and entertaining might be important for you. Are you a part-time evening student? You'll need study (quiet) space. Are you a newlywed? You'll need elbow room for your relationship. Are you a mother of young children? Time for yourself will be a priority. Are your children in their teens? Time for you and your husband to be alone together is crucial. Perhaps you are beginning to plan for retirement. Health, both physical and financial, may take priority.

Whatever your needs, give them priority. Otherwise, you will suffer, and so will your family and business.

Now that you've thought about your needs, think about the special things important to you. Do you need a sewing or painting area? How about a book nook for adults? What are your special pleasures? A creative outlet is important; you need space for it, too, or you'll be frustrated. It's especially important to save some private space for yourself, since you can easily feel overwhelmed by others and their demands. The time spent alone will rejuvenate and refresh you.

Another family member to consider is your spouse. Although not every provider is married, those who are must face the fact that their partner will have needs, too. Getting your attention may be the biggest frustration your spouse has. For example, if you are tied up on the phone with parents each night, it will have a bad effect on your relationship. The best solution is a clear separation between work and home time. When you're working, you won't be available. But when you're not, make time to do things together.

Early in my career, I got into the habit of running errands (during walks) or making calls (at naptime) for my husband. Then two things happened: my business started picking up and I became pregnant with my second child. By that time, my husband was used to asking me to do odds and ends for him. One day at lunchtime he called me from work. He asked me to find out the price of a motorcycle part in my spare time. I replied rather testily that I didn't have any more spare time than he did, and that if he was going to call me at work he could pick a more convenient time. Dinner that night was a bit strained, but I had made my point. However, I could have saved myself some trouble if I hadn't led him to expect those little extras in the first place.

To analyze your spouse's needs, think about that person's routine and note areas where your business might interfere. Consider your spouse's hobbies, relaxation time, and social life.

Ask your spouse to help you decide which activities are most important, and which require extra space. For many people, the idea of space as a valuable commodity is new. They are often unaware that the things they do can interfere with other people's activities. If, together, you choose spaces for your spouse's hobbies, work, and leisure activities, your spouse will remember to keep possessions there and not let them spill over into child care or others' spaces. And if your spouse doesn't often pick up, you can cultivate the habit of shutting the door on the space so nothing will be in the way.

Your children are another important part of the family to consider when planning your space. For many providers, a conflict exists between the needs of their own children and the needs of the clients' children. They fear showing favoritism to their own, but don't want to hurt them by ignoring their status in the group. The best approach is to acknowledge that they are extra special to you. Everyone realizes that you are more attached to your children, and trying to hide that will only confuse people. Make sure to be fair, however, and meet the needs of the other children. Reflect that fairness in the way you allocate space for the children. As a result, the resentment that the children feel towards each other will be minimal.

Even though your children may share the child care space, they will need a place to get away from your business. Also, think about how you will use space for them in off-business hours, and how you want to fulfill their needs and activities during off-business times like evenings and weekends.

I had a problem with Chelsea. On weekends, she loved having the playroom to herself; she knew she didn't have to share. But she would leave the toys lying around instead of putting them away. On Monday mornings, the place looked like it had been hit by a cyclone before the children had even arrived. The solution to our problem was teaching Chelsea that the picking-up rules applied, no matter what day of the week it was.

If you have infant children, you know that you are your baby's most important need, and he should be able to have you without waiting too long. This might mean a nursery monitor for naptime or a playpen used occasionally for toy room time. Your infant also needs a predictable schedule of naps, meals, and playtime and needs that schedule to be flexible. He needs access to his father and siblings as well. He needs special protection not only from hazards, but also from overstimulation. He needs his world to be safe and his space to be his own, with you only a moment away.

If you have a preschooler, keep in mind that she may have needs similar to the needs of your clients' children. Your preschooler, however, will also need to have access to you as her mom. Remember that she will be spending her days at home. She won't have the change of scene the other children have each day so she may get bored more easily. Get her out of the house a little each week. This will also give her a chance to develop her social skills. Remember, too, she needs a space all her own.

When Chelsea was three, she wanted her playmates to join her in her room at playtime. First, we let her have as many friends in her room as she wanted, which quickly led to overcrowding. Then we limited it to one friend at a time. This worked much better. She enjoyed the company, and she enjoyed being able to choose her company.

If you have school-age children, you don't necessarily have less problems. Many caregivers look forward to the day their own preschoolers start school. They expect that there will be less competition between their children and the clients' children when they spend less time together. But school occupies only 60 to 75 percent of the day. With school vacations and summers off, your child will still be home 80 percent of the time during the year. Be prepared for a little tension even after your children start school.

Schoolagers need space and your attention more than ever. When they get home, they'll be ready for a snack and your attention. They'll need time to play outside or to flop down in front of the TV. They'll need space to do their homework. You can also expect them to want to have their friends over, especially as they get older. They'll still enjoy companionship, if not hero-worship, from the younger children. But they may not have much patience.

Three-year-old Angie had been using the potty regularly. Then she began to backslide. It took a couple of days to figure out that she was afraid to go through my daughter's room to the bathroom. She had overheard Jean scolding another child who had touched something in her room. I asked Jean to be extra nice to her, and Angie began using the potty again.

If you have teenagers, you know that they are neither adults nor children; instead they're a little of each. Unfortunately, they rarely tell you which they will be at any given moment. Make sure you allow for both. They don't always realize that they might seem scary to the children when they wear extreme fashions, sulk, or become temperamental. They need an extra measure of privacy in which to do their growing up.

It's also important that they not be saddled with responsibility for the children. Teens are still close to childhood themselves, and they cannot handle that kind of responsibility. They are also not legally able to assume responsibility for unsupervised care of children.

A caregiver I knew was shocked when one of her clients accused her son of molesting a child. The son had the same name as the mother's boyfriend, and it turned out that the boyfriend was the real culprit. But because teen-age boys sometimes have been found to molest younger children, the caregiver's son was initially accused. The caregiver spent much time and money on legal services before his name was cleared.

Some teens just don't want anything to do with little ones. In this case, try to set up traffic patterns to keep children and teen apart.

Respecting the individuality of your teen is crucial when planning his space. Ask for his suggestions. At a calm moment (which may be hard to find), sit down together over a snack and ask for his ideas. Show him your plans and decide together how to work in the teen's space. If you treat your teen like an adult, you will be rewarded by their adult-like cooperation with your business' needs—at least some of the time!

If you have an adult child living at home, think about why they are at home as you list her needs. Is your child disabled in some way? Is she home temporarily while a spouse is in the service or house hunting? Is she employed? What is the goal for the adult child at home? Most have the plan of leaving, but occasionally a child can get too comfortable to move on. If you let them help you with the children, you may be subtly pressuring them to stay at home. If they take a role in your business, it should be recognized, and paid, just as it would be with anyone else.

Many caregivers care not only for children, but also for elderly or ill family members. This dual-caregiving role poses a dilemma for regulators. Does caring for an elderly, ailing parent take away attention from the children? Should the parent be counted in the ratio? What if the infirm person is not a relative, but a foster home placement?

When caring for an elderly or ill adult, health needs will be important. An infection caught from a child could harm this person more than it might harm a younger, healthy person. An older or ill person might also require more rest and quiet, and may need access to medications or other health supports. Think about that person's use of kitchen and bath, and stairways and walkways. Consider their interactions with children, and how well-oriented they are. If their social life is limited to the home, they will need company other than you and your clients. Craft your space carefully in order to avoid having that person feel like a prisoner in a world of noisy kids, traffic, and parents. They will need a sanctuary.

Sometimes, there may be an adult sharing living quarters with you for reasons other than health needs. If you have an adult living with the family, their needs for privacy and a routine will be important. They may also have less patience with the demands of your business, since they won't benefit from it directly, as a spouse or dependent child might. And the children will not benefit as much in knowing them as they might with an immediate family member, because their presence in the home is likely to be temporary.

In addition to their needs, consider their trustworthiness with the children. You might not want to facilitate too close a relationship between them and the children's parents, if the living arrangement is temporary. If this is a permanent arrangement, however, they'll need a clearly defined relationship with your business and clients.

Last but not least, you must consider the needs of pets. Pets are a wonderful addition to the home environment, but they need to sleep, eat, and play without trouble. They must be kept safe from the children (who might pull their tail or pick them up in an unsafe way); and the children must be protected from them as well (not only from scratches and bites, but also from animal-transmitted diseases, such as toxoplasmosis). Keep litter boxes and dog runs away from play areas and pet food out of reach or well guarded. Make sure parents know that their children are safe from your pet.

Never leave a baby or young child alone with a pet. Older children who know how to behave with a pet are a little safer, but a sudden noise or an accident can still cause pets to be aggressive with children. For that reason, your pet should be well supervised at all times with the children.

Our dog, Bet, was an energetic Lab-type mongrel who loved everyone, whether or not they wanted her love. When she was a puppy, the children couldn't get enough of her. During her first winter with us, I kept her indoors so that they could play together. As she got older, the children began to be afraid of her, so the next winter I made her an outdoor run with a shelter attached. Her playfulness was a little too rough for her to spend the day indoors. She was much happier chasing the squirrels than she was when she chased children.

Who are the other people to accommodate? Guests, repair people, renovators and builders, service people, your landlord, tax assessors—many people come into contact with your home; many might not think of it in terms of a business. You'll need to let them know, ahead of time if possible, that you have a business.

My pet peeve was unannounced visitors at naptime. To help eliminate this problem, I turned off the doorbell and hung a sign on the door asking visitors to come back after naptime. We also had a UPS delivery person who always seemed to show up just as the children were nodding off. He would pound loudly on the door until I answered it, which could take a while if I was diapering or rocking someone. I finally persuaded him that he would save us both a lot of trouble by leaving the package in our entry.

As you stay in business and your reputation spreads, you'll have to do less explaining and preparing of visitors, because people will already know that you are a child care provider.

Your Family's Activity Areas

The most important factor in planning the family's space is not what they do most urgently, but what they do most frequently. For instance, the most important thing you may do with your teen is a heart-to-heart talk once a week. If that talk is interrupted by a child, you have a weekly irritation. But if the most frequent thing you do with your teen is a quick rundown of what her day was like, you will need that time every school day, or five times a week. If that is interrupted, you will be irritated five times a week, which is harder to endure than a once-a-week interruption.

The most likely areas of conflict for activity areas are those that the family and the child care business have in common, like entry, toileting, phoning, or eating. If you can separate them, you will reduce friction. For example, your spouse shouldn't have to leapfrog over client families as he leaves for work in the morning. It's better to use separate entrances, or at least separate traffic patterns.

At the end of a long day, Michael looked forward to getting home around the time parents were picking up their children. His pet peeve was parents blocking the driveway so he couldn't get the car in the garage. (Although we had a driveway wide enough for two cars, it seemed that someone inevitably parked in the middle.) Usually, he was cordial about coming in, asking the parent to move the car, and going back out, sometimes in below-zero weather, to park. But once in a while, he'd lose his temper and blast the horn.

You'll need some planning to allow both your family members and child care children to enjoy mealtimes. Families don't usually enjoy eating with a collection of wistful eyes staring at them. They also may not enjoy the sight of children eating (drooling, spitting, fingering messy foods) as they relax over a meal. If you regularly care for children during family mealtimes, consider separating them at least occasionally. Use a room divider, closed door, or even a snacking space for family members in a bedroom.

The food your family eats can be a sensitive subject. Parents who want their children to have no sugar, for example, may be horrified to see you pouring syrup on your own children's waffles. And children in care will naturally want to partake in any treats they see your family enjoying. A good rule of thumb during business hours is to serve only those foods you are willing to share (or be sure the little ones don't see it).

Easter and Halloween candy were always treasured prizes in our house. And woe to the child who dared open someone else's box of Valentine chocolates. This less-than-generous attitude caused problems when the children spotted the goodies. Our solution was to make all treats off-limits during business hours, unless everyone could have a piece. To my surprise, this helped my children learn to share. They would rather pass around their candy than endure waiting for it. The children's parents usually tolerated the candy-eating well, since it only happened a few times each year. But if a parent objected, the candy was put out of sight until after-hours, and we shared a healthier treat instead.

The issue of rest is minor if you offer daytime child care and your family only sleeps at night. Your family probably has well-established sleeping space—the bedrooms. If you plan to use them for child care, too, be careful about how much space you use and when it is used. The person whose room is used should have a clear understanding about when they can have the room to themselves.

Sooner or later, however, someone in the family will get sick and need rest during business hours. Create a contingency plan.

I felt sorry for my husband when he was sick. He used to claim it was easier to be sick at work than to take a sick day at home. Not only did he need rest, he also needed chicken soup, and sometimes mindless TV. The best solution for us was to set up our bedroom as a sickroom, with everything he wanted. Then he did not have to shuffle through the kitchen, unshaven and in robe and slippers, to get an aspirin (usually needed just as families were arriving).

Planning for bathroom use is tough when you only have one bathroom and everyone shares. Separate space for some toileting activities (for example, applying makeup and hair drying) can help. Don't let the bathroom be used for anything that could be done elsewhere. Before-meal hand washing, for example, can be done at the kitchen sink just as well as in the bathroom (and it is easier to supervise as you prepare the meal, too). The family's bathroom should be as private as possible, away from traffic and child care space.

During our giardiasis epidemic, bathroom use was tricky. Faucets and toilet surfaces had to be disinfected between each use to prevent the spread of the microscopic parasite, but my family wouldn't bother to disinfect. Since we were lucky enough to have two bathrooms, I designated the upstairs bath as the non-giardiasis bath. Only those found to be free of the parasite could use it, and less cumbersome sanitation was acceptable. Children who had not yet been tested or were being treated used the downstairs bathroom, and the more rigorous cleaning practices were observed. This made my job easier, and reduced the chance of contagion. (These were the health practices suggested by the Health Department at the time of the illness. Practices may have changed or your local Health Department may recommend other practices.)

When family and child care must share an entry area, efficiency and ease are the top priorities. Do everything you can to reduce traffic jams in the doorway. Don't store family outerwear near children's cubbyholes and hooks. Leave enough room between the door and children's storage so that families will not set children and possessions down in the doorway to say good-bye. Use family outerwear storage for outerwear only; sports equipment and other items will only contribute clutter.

If you use a corridor or walkway as an area for wheeled toys, stow away the toys during high-traffic times.

It's hard enough if your spouse leaves for work at the same time families arrive. If your children are leaving for school, too, it's even more difficult for things to go smoothly. Do your family and yourself a favor by making sure that everything is ready for departure the night before. And don't forget, in the flurry of arriving clients, that your own children need a kiss and hug good-bye.

Remember that older children and adults in your family need space to prepare for school or work. They also need safe storage for the items they'll use. Once again, separation is desirable. It's hard to concentrate on studying or completing a project while a little one is pestering you. A work area away from the traffic is best, but if your children insist on doing their homework at the kitchen table (as mine did), it may be wise to shut down children's activities in the kitchen near the end of the day. Use the children's activity areas in the rest of the house instead.

Jean was in the school band for several years. She was required to practice her flute for twenty minutes four times a week. The younger children found the noise scary, and the older children were so intrigued by her playing that they pestered her for a turn on the flute. We needed to get her away from them so she could concentrate. Our final solution was seasonal. In winter, she practiced in her room with the door closed as the children watched "Sesame Street" (which drowned out the muffled sound of the flute). During warm weather, she practiced outdoors, to the delight of the neighbors.

Your family's home is more than just a pit stop where members go when they need food, sleep, and clean clothes. They do things there: pursue hobbies, be creative, play. They need space for relaxation and recreation.

Whether your family watches TV, plays cards, has friends over, or listens to music, try to accommodate what the family enjoys. Some families are TV fans, so a special, isolated spot for the television is important. Some prefer sports, and need storage space for equipment and a place to practice. Others may have a wide circle of friends and need a place to visit with them. Recreation is different for each family, and you may need several areas to give everyone enough space.

Even if your family and you do not especially enjoy exercise, we all need some, and it can take up space. Do you have an exercise bike, rowing machine, or other exercise equipment? Do your children have gymnastics equipment or active toys? These will not be used if you don't have the space for them, so remember to plan for it.

Like the children in your child care, your family needs to know that their things are respected; they need storage space for their personal things. Your teen won't like coming home from school to find her makeup spread all over her room (and she'll lose no time in letting you know it). Your spouse will not admire the children's creativity if they redecorate a collection of first-edition books. What's worse, your spouse will probably be tempted to share his feelings with their parents in no uncertain terms. Avoid disasters like these by planning for the safety of your family's possessions.

This living room storage unit keeps family possessions out of reach, while children's toys and books are handy.

Perhaps your family might look something like the Smiths. We'll use them and their needs as a basis for the activity areas listed below. (We'll also discuss these needs in the home layout section in Chapter 4.)

Name	Age	Needs
Sharon	30 yrs.	a break when the children are napping; study time and space for night class; a walk or other exercise after work
Stu	31 yrs.	privacy in the mornings; time and space for home computer; room for power tools and workbench
Tony	8 yrs.	homework help; time to watch TV after school; space for his elaborate erector set; time to learn not to tease the younger children
Jenny	6 yrs.	privacy for her bed-wetting problem; dress-up time; space for her special collection of rocks and twigs; time to overcome her jealousy of the children in care

Sample Activity Areas for the Smiths

Transition/Entry	one area is needed
Meals	two: one indoor and one outdoor
Recreation	six: one for TV, one for Stu's workshop, one for visiting with friends, one for Tony's erector set, one for Jenny's dress-up clothes, and one for her nature collection
Toileting	one
Exercise	one indoor and one outdoor
Sleep	three: one for Sharon and Stu; one for each child
Work	four: one for Sharon's schoolwork, one for each child's homework, and one for Stu's computer

The Wild Card

Families are an unpredictable lot. Just like your child care constellation, your family constellation will change, sooner or later. You can't always tell when someone will get married, have children, become ill, or die. There will be special events (including short- and long-term entertaining); renovations or repairs to the structure of the house; and family events such as reunions, communions, weddings, graduations, christenings or *bris*. Children grow up; their interests change. Marriages ripen or end. Rifts and reunions surprise us with happy or unhappy endings.

This is the stuff of life and can bring joy or sorrow. These things can also wreak havoc on your carefully thought-out space plans. That's the time to remember that your space plan is only a tool, and it can only be as flexible as you are. So when your family throws you a curve, see it as a new challenge, not an annoyance. Life brings change, and change is easier when you've learned to accept and embrace it.

Your Space

In the first three chapters, we focused on people, including your child care and family constellations. There's one more item to think about before you improve your use of home space: the space itself.

Before you make changes, look at the space your activity areas will occupy. Although each home is unique, some qualities are common to all spaces. We will discuss these qualities, or attributes, and how they affect your activity areas. Then we will look at a few sample floor plans, and how they could be used for activities.

How Your Space Feels to Your Family and Children in Care

The attributes of space are qualities that define what that space feels like. The qualities do not refer to decor but to the physical properties of the space. If you use the physical properties to your advantage, you'll find that children will use your activity areas the way you want them to be used.

Light, sound, ventilation, temperature, openness, and accessibility are the main attributes of space.

Light

"In the beginning there was darkness, and on the first day God created light." This biblical story is just one example of how important light has been throughout history. Ancient civilizations worshipped the sun; and the winter solstice has long been the occasion of celebration. More recently, researchers have found that exposure to increased light can relieve some types of depression.

Many states have child care lighting requirements, measured in foot-candles, usually near the floor (where children see). Sufficient lighting is not only an esthetic and practical concern, but also a safety one. Make sure traffic areas, especially stairs and walkways, have sufficient light.

Light is needed for nearly all family and child care activities. But not all light is created equal. Daylight shifts throughout the day and differs from season to season. Light can be cold (fluorescent light or winter sun) or warm (incandescent and warm-white fluorescent artificial light or summer sun).

Light can also be even or focused. For many activities, an even, overall brightness is preferred. In natural light, north light is the most even (many artists prefer to work in studios with windows on the north wall). In southern, western, or eastern light, colors and shadows change more as the sun crosses the sky. Focused light can dramatically emphasize an area or create a warm, intimate feeling, depending on whether it is bright or dim.

When you plan your activity areas, consider the amount and kind of light that will be present throughout the day and year. Adequate summertime light on a porch or in a garage may not be enough in winter. And winter sun is lower in the sky, so it will shine into your house at a different angle. Think also about how cloudy your area tends to be. And remember, the days are shorter in winter, so you will need to compensate with artificial light in some areas.

Of course, darkness is desirable at some times, when children are napping, for example. But even then you will not want total darkness (which may scare the children), but a low, warm light. Room-darkening shades can do the trick. Insulated curtains can also dim the light, and help keep the room warmer, too. For some types of play (ghost games, hide-and-seek) areas of dim light are important. And dim light can also feel like a retreat from stimulation, so offer that option in a cuddling area. Make sure that it can be brighter when you want a more inviting feel, for more than one person to share. A lamp with a dimmer or a three-way bulb works well.

Consider setting up your lighting so preschool children can control it. That will save you steps and provide them with a sense of being in control.

When Chelsea was three, she became afraid of the dark. Even her night-light was not enough to calm her. If we kept the overhead light on, however, it shone in her eyes and kept her awake. The solution that worked for us was to install a dimmer on her light switch. At bedtime, she set the light the way she wanted it, and her fears lessened.

You can affect the appearance of light through decorating. Use cool colors where light is overly bright and warm. Use yellows, yellow-based greens, or light oranges in spaces where light is cool. The colors will reflect on the areas around them and alter the feel of the space. Space that is cluttered will seem darker, so use light colors to compensate. For instance, the lower level of a split-level home is often paneled with dark wood. As a play area, however, it absorbs too much light. Below ground level, use warm, light colors. A light-colored floor, even though it may show the dirt more, gives a cleaner appearance than a dark one.

Light, neutral colors that retreat into the background and have a calming influence are good in high-traffic, noisy areas. Busy patterns, such as rugs with numbers and letters all over them, are distracting. They look cute in catalogs, but are exhausting to live with. Jim Greenman, author of the excellent child care center environment book *Caring Spaces, Learning Places: Children's Environments That Work*, provides a good rule of thumb: If you wouldn't want it in your living room, don't use it for children, either. Busy patterns cause kids and adults to use up energy tuning out the environment.

Don't neglect the outdoors, although in some places you may have to block, reduce, or soften light. To control light outside, use awnings, tents and tarps, shade plants (remember seasonal changes), latticework and trellises, gazebos, porches, and playhouses. Sometimes you will have to add light, as in the winter when it gets dark around 4 p.m. Safety, as well as aesthetics, becomes a concern. Use outdoor lamp lights or turn on the garage and porch lights. For a fun touch, use holiday lights in generous amounts; the children will love playing under them. Make sure arriving parents can see children playing outside, and vice versa, to avoid accidents.

Sound

Noise can be loud or soft, steady (waves on a beach) or intermittent (the ringing of a telephone). It can be soothing or a source of annoyance. Noise can pollute just like odors can. For example, a radio or television playing all day will overstimulate children, annoy adults, and inhibit language development and conversation.

A little noise is good; it lets you and others know what is going on in the house and helps to orient children. But too much, too loud, or too constant noise can be bad. People use up energy just to tune out the noise. That is why it's not good to yell at children all the time; after a while, they don't even hear you. (If you save your loud voice for certain occasions, such as warning of a danger that seems imminent, they will respond much better.)

Some activities are noisy and should take place in an area where that will not disturb anyone. Other activities, such as reading or napping, require quiet. All other things being equal, it will help your organization and your sanity if the noisy activities take place on the periphery, and the quiet ones are close by. You'll be able to hear the noisy ones even if you can't see them all the time.

When you plan your activity areas, don't put quiet and noisy activities in adjacent space. Keep in mind what the existing level of noise is before activities begin, and what sorts of sounds will likely happen there. Below ground level tends to be quieter; the road side of a house tends to be noisier, as does the space around a teen's room. Muffle rooms where noisy activities take place to avoid echoes. Curtains, rugs, and tapestries make good sound insulators; so do cardboard boxes and egg cartons stapled onto the wall (if you don't care about the wall). Cushion doorjambs with weather stripping, and oil hinges, windows, and cabinet hardware to cut down on squeaks. Where quiet activities such as listening to music or stories happen, don't let background noise compete with the activity.

You may want two kinds of dramatic play areas, one noisy (rock stars, Teenage Mutant Ninja Turtles) and one quiet (housekeeping, doctor). It can be tempting to set up quiet activity areas inside and noisy ones outdoors. But in a stretch of bad weather you need to be able to let kids be noisy inside. Also, your neighbors may not appreciate having only the noisy activities outside.

Channel the children's natural tendency to be noisy into appropriate activities and space. Set up space so they can be noisy when they need to be, and so other children and family members can get away from it.

Ventilation

Good ventilation is essential for health and relieves any closed-in feelings. Children get more colds in winter because of decreased air circulation that allows germs to accumulate, not because the outside air is cold.

 I aired out my home in the winter by leaving the doors open at least twice a week for about ten minutes. The fresh air was revitalizing. I figured what we lost in heat, we gained in health.

Ventilate small spaces, such as playhouses, cuddle areas, or napping alcoves. If you count on windows for air circulation, make sure they can be opened but not climbed out of. Be aware of possible release of toxic fumes such as car exhaust or cleaning-solvent fumes. Try using fans mounted at the tops of doorways or ceiling fans to help move stale air around.

Many children are allergic to airborne dust mites, pollen, or ashes, so vacuum regularly. Avoid deep-pile carpeting and upholstery, where dust accumulates. Change air filters on furnaces frequently or use electrostatic filters. In a tightly-insulated home, use an air exchanger. Be sure to test your home for radon infiltration.

Smell is part of ventilation, too. The sense of smell is our most primal, and we react emotionally to smells even when we are unaware of them. Don't try to eradicate homey smells that are inviting, such as kitchen smells. They help make your home special. In bathrooms, however, install a vent fan if you don't have a window or can't keep a window open year-round. Work to rid your house of mustiness or smoke. Be aware of how areas and surfaces smell, especially those that people lie or sit on. Cushions or beds smelling of stale urine or sweat are not appealing. The smell of stale cigarette smoke is also distasteful.

Temperature

You want your home to be warm and inviting, and sufficient heating and cooling are necessary to accomplish this. Children and adults must be comfortable in order to pursue their activities. Some states even set child care guidelines for minimum and/or maximum temperatures, both indoors and outdoors. Remember, temperature at adult height is warmer than at child height, because heat rises. So test your home's temperature on the floor, if you are caring for infants, and one foot off the floor for older children. The temperature should be no lower than 65 degrees Fahrenheit; 67 to 70 degrees is better.

A few accessories and your decor can help your home's temperature feel more comfortable. Use afghans to snuggle under in cold weather; handheld fans to cool off with in summer. To warm up your home, throw a patchwork quilt or wool shawl over your sofa; put down a few bright throw rugs (watch out for slippery ones); or set a bowl of gourds and pumpkins on the table. During the summer, help your house feel cool by installing light, airy window coverings; leaving space open on shelves and walls; and keeping the floors bare.

Don't use temperature as an excuse to stay inside. For children who can crawl or walk, 20 degrees (including windchill) is still warm enough to enjoy outdoor play if they are warmly dressed. Babies, bundled warmly and set in a wind-protected, sunny corner of a porch or patio will enjoy the outdoors, too. Have a stash of spare outerwear (including boots) stored near the entry area just in case.

In my part of the country, there is a fifth season: mud season (between winter and spring). Our dirt-and-gravel driveway was a source of constant fascination for the children at that time of year. They dug and molded the mud into numerous shapes and concoctions. More than once the mud was soft and deep enough to pull a child's boot right off his foot. Fortunately, we were always able to retrieve the boots. We had five extra pairs and at least that many pairs of mittens, used more often in mud season than in winter. Even so, we ran out of mittens as the children played in muddy slush. In a pinch, I put heavy socks on their hands. It worked.

Use a small space in your garage or other sheltered space for a break from the indoors in winter, if it's too cold to take them out. They will love coming back into your warm, inviting house for some cocoa and toast after a play session outside.

After three or four winter months, we always developed a case of cabin fever. One day I couldn't stand the thought of another minute in the house, but it was 10 degrees below zero outside. We decided to have a beach party. I turned the heat up to 85 degrees, the children stripped down to their underwear, and I put our wading pool on the kitchen floor (surrounded by towels and a thick layer of newspapers). We added warm water, bubbles and toys, and put a Beach Boys cassette into the tape player. After an hour or so of splashing around, we had a picnic-style lunch on the dining room floor. The children slept better that afternoon than they had in days! And I felt more relaxed than I had for days, too. That activity proved to me that sometimes you have to be a little crazy to hang on to your sanity.

In hot weather, on the other hand, use plenty of fans (out of the children's reach) if you don't have air conditioning. Keep in mind the cooling properties of water and offer water play to the children daily. In hot weather, make it an all-day option. Sprinklers and water pistols are safer and less germy than pools. Outdoors, have plenty of shade and drinking water. If children can get to the drinking water without your help, you will save steps and teach the children independence.

Openness

It's not easy to dance in a closet. But that's how your space will feel to the children if you plan activity areas that require large, sweeping space in an area filled with knickknacks or clutter. On the other hand, a bare, stark room can be almost forbidding, and no one wants to cuddle, socialize, or rest in such a place. The ideal is to tailor your space to the kind of activities that will happen in it.

Children feel safe in small, enclosed spaces.

Have a variety of spaces available. Open spaces, free of clutter, invite large muscle activities. Other spaces that have a little useful clutter (interesting things to look at, pillows and upholstery to rest on, toys and books) invite children to linger for a while. Spaces that feel too closed in can be opened up either physically or by rearranging objects. In the areas where children spend much time, make sure they can see out of the windows. If the windows are too high, put climbable furniture or platforms in front of them. Make sure they can't climb out of the windows, however.

Low windows that let light in and let children see out are best.

The space around your television is important. Because you want to be able to control how inviting the TV is, don't face it into a big open space where it intrudes on other activities. You also don't want it to dominate your cozy space. Instead, put the television off in a corner by itself, facing a limited range of space furnished with comfortable seating. Those who are watching it can do so without disturbing, or being disturbed by, others.

Nap space should be cozy and inviting but not too closed in and claustrophobic. Having the children sleep in a large open room, especially with a high ceiling, can inhibit relaxation. Each child should have her own nook to sleep in.

You will need some small, cozy space outside. Infants between 4 and 18 months can find outdoor, wide-open spaces threatening. Use a small enclosed space, such as a tent, sheltered porch, or playhouse.

I wanted a private space outdoors for the children and a place for them to play house. We made a project of building our own playhouse in a five-foot high area under our deck. The children helped me design it, parents donated much of the building supplies, and we all worked together (which is to say the children tried to help, and I did most of the work). We painted (messy but fun) and furnished it with toy furniture, crates for seats, and curtains. When everything was completed, we had a "playhouse warming" and a potluck cookout after work one Friday. The children and their families enjoyed the accomplishment of the playhouse-building, and everyone shared in the excitement of seeing it really happen. Some families even brought housewarming gifts, like toy dishes and a toy phone. The children used the playhouse for many of their games, even in the winter.

Accessibility

This is the most complex space quality and your major tool for crowd and traffic control. Here's a basic rule of thumb: If you want someone to be able to get to something easily, make it accessible, if not, don't. Of course, this rule works differently for adults than children (for example, high shelves for purses or keys).

Use moveable or permanent barricades to keep children out of places they don't belong. When you're planning space that will be accessible to the children, get down on their level (that is, on your knees, or flat on the floor, depending on the age of the child) to determine what it will look like to them. (While you're at it, look at an adult from that viewpoint and see how powerful we look to children.)

For all of your spaces, consider accessibility in terms of how easy an area is to get to and leave. Remember to consider the parents' needs, especially drop-off and pickup, which are hectic enough without additional hurdles. Parking should be easy and safe.

The entrance should be well lit and as spacious as possible; this is a good place to avoid clutter. If the entrance needs "warming up," hang children's artwork or other items on the walls. Keep in mind that the main function here is practical, not aesthetic. A child care home with a small entrance that is shared by family and business is no place for an umbrella stand or elaborate antique clothes tree.

Some items, like electronic equipment, should not be reachable by children.

Outdoors, accessibility is not only an issue of convenience for clients and family, but also one of security. Your vigilance is the most important safeguard. But don't overlook other safety measures: door locks, peepholes in doors, intercom systems for entries, convex mirrors placed strategically outside so you can see all of the property from one position, fencing, and quick access to the telephone.

Sample Homes with Activity Areas

When you plan activity areas, keep in mind the individuality of the children in your care. In Chapter 2, seven children—Mark, Brenda, Carl, Annette, Deena, Brendon, and Lydia—and their concerns were listed. A caregiver planning a space for this group would have to keep in mind their different age groups and their very different needs.

There should be a place for Mark's mother to breast-feed him in privacy. His play and napping spaces should be separate from other activity areas (both for protection from the other children and because his schedule varies so much) and far from noisy activity areas. In the entry area, he and Annette should have adjacent cubbyholes and hooks.

Brenda should have a nook out of view of the other children to use for her morning snack. Because of her biting fears, the dog should be kept away from areas she uses. There should be a book area for language development, including books, toy phones, and walkie-talkies, and a housekeeping area to encourage Brenda's normal speech development and help with Annette's lagging speech.

There should be another dramatic play area, too, to accommodate Brendon's Superman games and other noisier pretendings. Deena's need for physical activities and

Lydia's love of the outdoors should be provided for in the indoor and outdoor gym areas. Annette should have a cuddling space so she can snuggle with the caregiver and other children and a privacy area so she can have the option of being alone when she gets frustrated. Privacy areas are also needed for Brendon, when he needs to get away from Carl's pestering; Lydia, when she needs a break from the stimulation of school or wants to read in peace; and Carl, when he loses his temper and needs a place to cool off.

In an art/manipulatives area, Deena would need a special area for her Barbie games, out of smaller children's reach. Brendon would also need space there for quiet play while the younger children are napping.

The sample family mentioned in Chapter 3 has activities, too. Those family members (Sharon, Stu, Tony, and Jenny) should also be accounted for in any space planning. Sharon would need space to study for her class; Stu would need a place for a workshop; Tony would need a safe place to store his erector set; and Jenny would need an area to play dress up and store her nature collection.

Following are the activity areas planned for in the sample house plans (these areas were discussed in detail in Chapters 2 and 3):

Indoor child care areas, including transition/entry, meals, rest, toileting, cuddling, privacy, gym, small manipulatives, book nook, dramatic play, art and music, exploration, sensory play, and TV.

Outdoor child care areas, including meals, cuddling, privacy, gym, small manipulatives, art and music, exploration, and sensory play.

Adult business areas, including office/meeting, entry, parking, special events, and observation.

Indoor family areas, including transition/entry, meals, recreation, toileting, exercise, sleep, and work.

Outdoor family areas, including meals, recreation, exercise, and work. The following sample homes are set in spaces that would challenge many caregivers. Although they represent worst-case scenarios in terms of available space, few compromises have been made. The homes presented here are small (the cape style home, the largest example, is only 896 square feet, measured externally; that means the square footage includes closets, corridors, interior walls, and other fixtures). The smallest, an apartment, is a mere 416 square feet.

The activity area plans are based on actual, existing child care homes. In planning spaces, each caregiver observed a few general rules that made a critical difference.

1. Less is more. Keep furniture, especially upholstered furniture, to a minimum. The following sample homes have only one sofa and armchair in the living room and one upholstered chair in the bedroom. Coffee tables either serve double duty or are not welcome. Bureaus are space-consumers; better to invest in space-wise closet storage using bins, shelves, and stacking drawers alongside hanging clothes. (If money is tight, you can accomplish wonderful space saving with sturdy cardboard boxes stacked sideways and open at one end; that way, you don't need to buy plastic or wire bins and shelving.)

2. Small is beautiful. Small children feel safe in small spaces; keep your activity areas cozy. Furniture should be modest sized, too; queen-sized not king-sized beds; moderate-sized dining tables (if you entertain a lot, consider buffet-style dinners). Use infant feeding chairs secured to sturdy tables; high chairs take up too much room.

3. Spread up if you can't spread out. Storage is easy if you add shelving right up to the ceiling, over beds, meal/art areas, and desks.

4. Keep mobile. Locking-type casters under furniture allow you to move the items around, which gives you loads of furniture arrangements that don't involve heavy lifting.

5. Be a miser about space—every square inch counts. Sell or give away what you don't need. Keep purchases to a minimum, and enjoy the peacefulness of a simple, uncluttered home.

6. Make furniture do double duty. A sensory (water or sand) table becomes a bench when covered with a decorated lid that locks. A rustic bench may serve as a coffee table in country-decor homes.

Sample Home 1: A Small Two-Story Cape

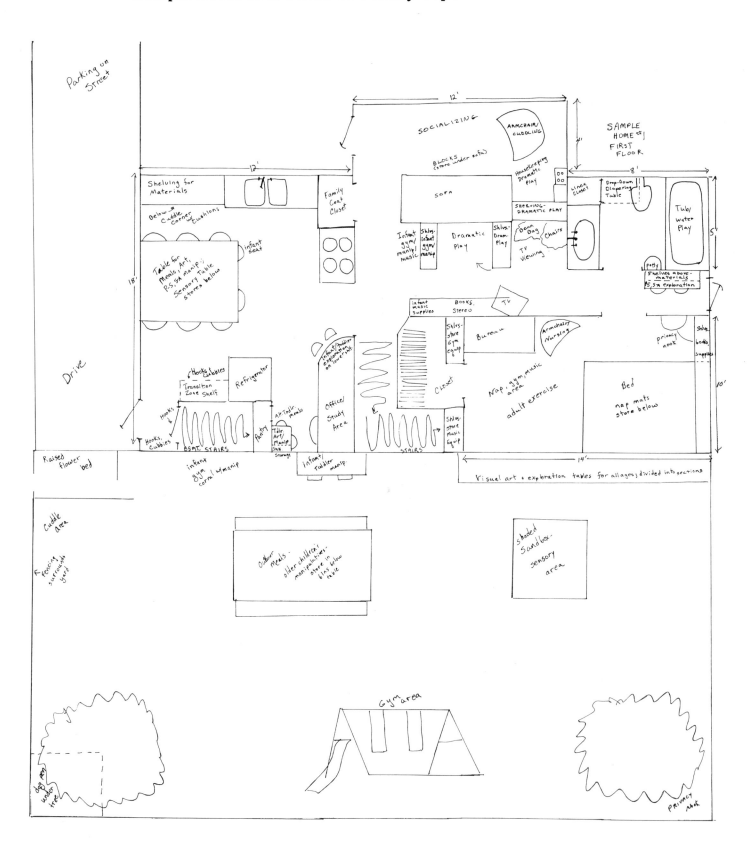

This small home has two entrances, one for family and one for child care. Hooks and cubbies lead from the back door into the kitchen, where parents can sit to dress children. Meals, art, and manipulatives are enjoyed at the table, too; adjacent shelving holds materials and overhangs a cozy cuddling space. A sensory table (box on wheels filled with sand or rice) slides out from under the kitchen table when needed. The work triangle of stove, refrigerator, and sink is open space. A nook behind cellar stairs accommodates pantry, office/study space, and a tiny toddler table for small manipulatives and the occasional private snack. Shelving above office and toddler space houses supplies. At the end of the office area counter, an infant/toddler exploration area with low shelving and pint-sized stools waits for action.

Around the corner in the living room, a sofa and easy chair create adult socializing space near the family entrance. During the day, block trays slide out from under the sofa for play; a housekeeping play area is tucked behind an armchair (the armchair is an alternate cuddling area). Behind the sofa, an infant gym-manipulatives-music area is separated from a second dramatic play area by shelving that stores dramatic play props. Beyond that, and behind a second small shelving unit, is a TV viewing space furnished with small beanbag chairs. Since the shelving units are on casters, they can be turned at night to form sofa back tables and side tables, handy because there is no coffee table. For special occasions, the shelves and upholstered furniture can "back up" to create more space. All TV, stereo, books, and infant play supplies are stored on shelving along the back wall.

Beyond the living room, the bathroom provides toileting space along with water play. A drop-down diaper-changing shelf offers convenience and sanitation next to the sink.

In the hall outside the bathroom, near a third exit, is an exploration space for three year olds and up; the shelves above store rock, pinecone, and other collections. Beyond the hall is the master bedroom, which is used for gym play by older children, and adult exercise after hours. An armchair provides nursing space. Musical instruments and tapes are nearby and stored on shelves near the closet. Next to the bed is a privacy nook; nap mats are stored under the bed until it is time for rest. Shelves over the bed eliminate the need for night tables and provide extra storage.

Hint: Often the most practical layout involves placing a bed along a wall. Don't drive yourself nuts trying to make a bed in the traditional way if you do place your beds along the wall. Consider using duvets (sheet-pocketed comforters) and light sleeping bags that open up to become spreads for you and your children. Both are easily laundered and neither needs to be tucked in under the mattress.

Sample Home 1: Second-Floor

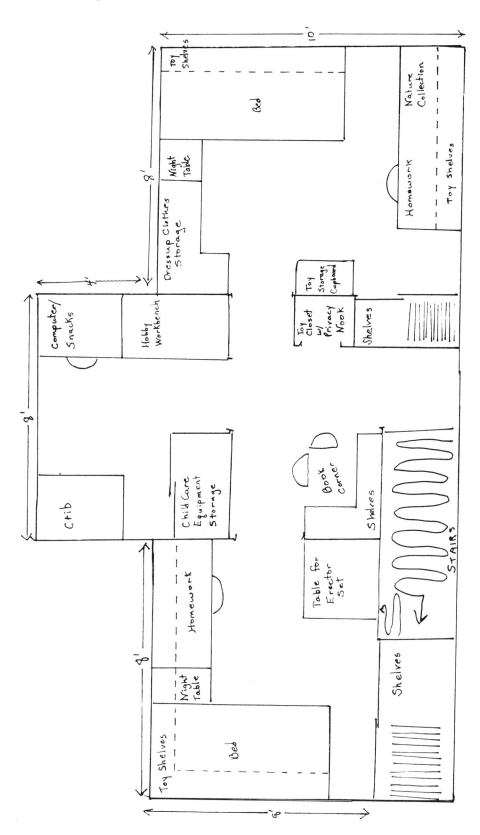

Upstairs, a book nook is tucked around the landing opposite a doorless closet. The closet's bottom half is a privacy nook; above, shelves hold supplies. Two bedrooms are at opposite sides of the landing; using closet bin storage instead of bureaus saves space in both rooms. The third tiny room houses an infant crib, computer desk with eating space for hideaway meals, and a hobby workbench. A closet holds additional children's equipment and toys out of circulation.

Outside, a raised flower bed provides a visual barrier from the driveway, and play areas are spread throughout the yard. The dog has a pen in a corner under a shady tree.

Sample Home 2: A Second-Floor Apartment

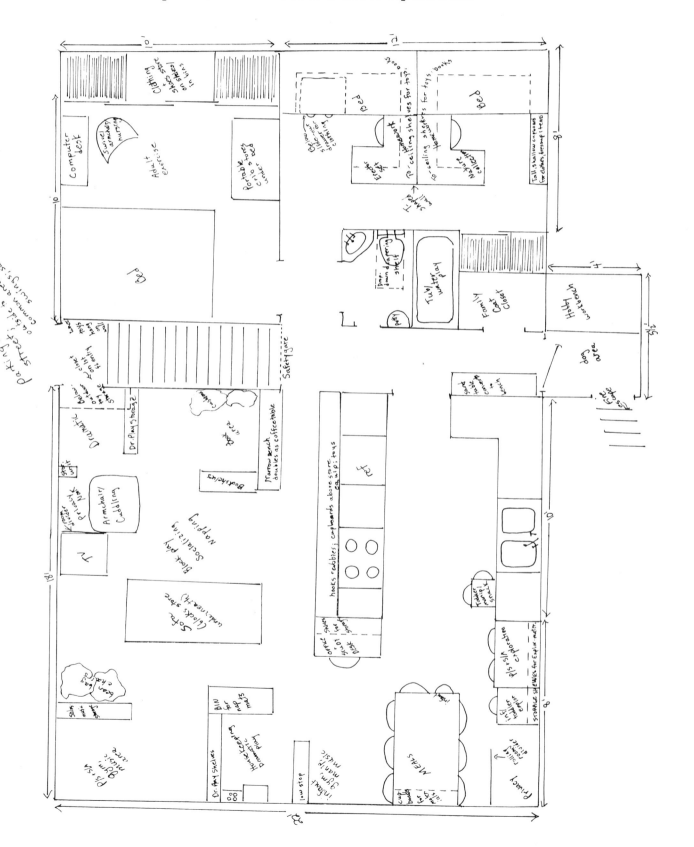

A closet at the bottom of the stairs holds the outdoor equipment, which must be set up and taken down rather than left out. The equipment includes low folding tables, which offer art and meals space, and a large shopping cart, which totes toys and supplies. Bikes and other wheel toys, along with a folding stroller, hang from sturdy hooks high on the wall. (Permanent sandbox and swings are set up for the apartment complex.) The stair wall serves as an art display area.

A safety gate at the top of the stairs stands guard; hooks, cubbies, and storage shelves line the wall nearest the living room (heavy curtains close at night to shield these from view). Opposite, a bench offers seating; at night, it can be turned around and used as a coffee table. The bench and a small bookcase behind it serve as a book area. In the corner, two other shelf units, one small and one large, flank the dramatic play area. Beyond, along the wall, is a tiny privacy nook, bordered by the back of an armchair and a room divider. The television is on the other side of the divider, facing a small pile of cushions. It is flanked by the side of the sofa. In front of the sofa is an open area that serves for block play (blocks are stored on trays under the sofa). Behind the sofa, shelves separate gym and housekeeping dramatic play areas. The shelves are on casters for quick conversions to adult entertaining.

A large rolling bin flanks the housekeeping area and holds nap mats; if covered, it could serve as a side table or buffet. A low carpeted step separates the housekeeping area from the infant gym-manipulative-music area; the step opens like a box to store accessories for these activities. Opposite the infant area is the caregiver's office and study desk with shelving for storage above. Beyond is the meals area, also used for art and manipulatives. Materials for these are stored in cupboards on the wall over the table's end. Beyond, along the kitchen wall, a privacy nook is tucked into the corner, protected by a room divider. It faces an infant/toddler exploration area: a low bench with nature items. Next is a higher desk with seating for older children's exploration area; materials are stored above on shelves. A tiny table and chairs for toddler manipulatives and snack can be slid out when needed and is stored under the dining table.

Through the kitchen and to the right, a narrow, sensory table doubles as a bench. Beyond, an enclosed porch holds workbench and pets. Facing the sensory table is the family coat closet. Down the hall, the bathroom offers diapering on a fold-down shelf over the toilet and next to the sink. The tub offers water play and a potty chair waits nearby. Around the corner, the caregiver's two children share a room that is divided by a T-wall ending at a walkway to the closet where both store hanging clothes. Shelves line the T-wall and exterior walls for storage; U-shaped desks with small swivel chairs offer homework and hobby space. One child stores her real and dress-up clothes in a tall shallow cupboard next to the foot of her bed. The other child stores his clothes in an oversized drawer on casters that slides out from under his bed.

In the master bedroom across the hall, a portable crib folds to store under the bed. A wall-long closet houses hanging and folding clothes and shoes. An armchair near the computer desk accommodates a nursing mom.

Sample Home 3: A Mobile Home

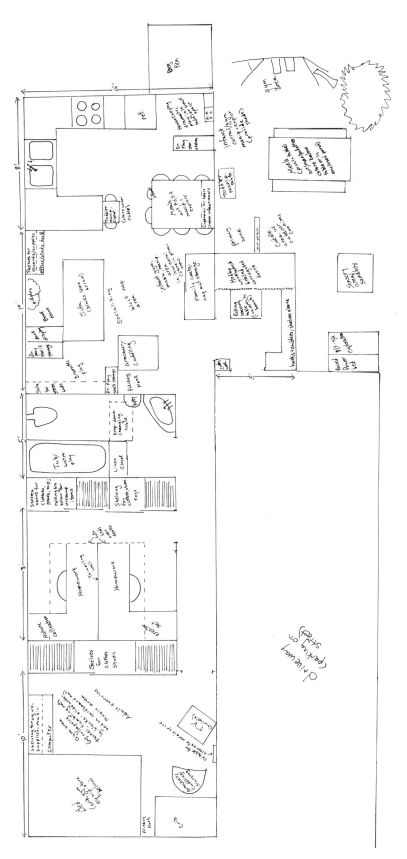

This small, 575 square foot home is especially challenging because 42.5 square feet are used up by a hall. The small enclosed porch serves as a transition area, with hooks and cubbies. A sensory table on casters doubles as a bench when the padded lid is closed. The table backs toward the door on weekends and provides seating for the hobby workbench at one end of the porch (corrugated doors conceal the workbench during business hours).

The family coat closet beyond the front door stores nap mats, too. An infant gym, music, and manipulative area is in front; cushions or low bolsters protect the area from traffic. At night, these things store in the privacy area tucked behind an armchair; the privacy area is backed by a shelf unit that faces the dramatic play area and provides storage for dramatic play props. A sofa side and another shelving unit also border the dramatic play area. Stereo equipment is housed on shelving above. Behind the sofa, the back of the dramatic play shelving unit serves to display books for the cushion-lined book nook. In the opposite corner, the caregiver's desk offers study and office space. Under the sofa, blocks are stored on trays that slide out front for play; the trays are decorated with block shapes to encourage children to sort them by size, shape, or color. An armchair provides cuddling space, and the sofa and chair are socializing areas for family and friends after hours. Shelf units and furniture roll back along walls to accommodate larger gatherings; all are on locking casters.

The dining table, used for art and older children's manipulatives and exploration, flanks the kitchen entrance; materials for these areas are stored in cupboards over the table. Opposite, a tiny toddler table and chairs offer space for toddler manipulatives and exploration; they slide under the larger table after hours or during adult gatherings. In a corner beyond the dining table, the housekeeping dramatic play area is bordered by the refrigerator and storage shelf unit; this space offers a toddler snack space option, too.

Down the hall, the bathroom offers water play at the tub; materials are stored in shallow wire baskets supported along the back tub wall by spring rods. A potty chair is near the sink; a step stool is underneath the sink. A drop-down changing table on the side of the linen closet is adjacent to the sink.

Next door in the children's room, an added wall separates children's space, leaving a walkway for access to closets and the far side of the room. Lofts provide sleep space; L-shaped desks below offer homework and hobby space. A roll-out chest on one side of the closet stores dress-up clothes. Both children have two feet of hanging clothes space; the remainder of the closet is divided by shelves and cubbies, eliminating the need for bureaus.

In the master bedroom, a computer desk next to the bed offers alternate snack space. Shelves above it and above both bed walls offer storage. The gym and music area is next to the bed. A collapsing tunnel, tumbling mats, and large blocks slide under the bed on shallow cardboard trays for easy access and storage. Adult exercise after hours uses the same space. The portable crib stands in the corner behind the armchair; it can fold to store under the foot of the bed if desired. Between the crib and the bed is just enough space for another tiny privacy nook. The armchair provides breast-feeding comfort; the television faces the chair and bed for viewing.

Hint: If baby is sleeping, the caregiver or schoolagers could still watch a video or a show by using headphones with the television.

Designing Your Plan

As you've read through the chapters of this book, you've considered the needs and activities of each child in your care, the children's families, and other professional contacts. You've also considered the needs and activities of your own family and those who visit or use your home. You've made a point to think about your own needs and activities, giving them special priority because of how important you are to both child care and family.

You've also started to think about the kind of space you need for the activity areas of your business and household. You've realized the importance of light, sound, and texture. You have a clear understanding of how important the environment of your home is to the activities and the people in your home. In this chapter, you will use your new knowledge and understanding to design the ideal space for your child care home. You are now ready to bring it all together.

If you already know some of the changes you need to make, try them out as soon as you wish. It's not necessary to go through this chapter before making any changes. You will find if you follow the steps in this chapter, the process of reorganizing space will be easy, flexible, and fun.

Before You Begin

Following are a few reminders to keep you on track as you begin your home design. These reminders will give you a perspective of creativity that will help you to find your own design.

- Your home and possessions are just tools that you will use to achieve your goals. They will be the instruments of your success, and you can use them any way you want. Forget what you've called the rooms up until now; give them new names and new roles. Instead of a laundry room, you might have a water room where laundry, a water table, bubble play, and wet play clothes peacefully coexist. Instead of a bedroom, you might have a quiet room for sleeping, cuddling, reading, and listening to quiet music. As a warm-up exercise, list the rooms in your home. Now list alternative uses for those rooms. A few ideas from other providers might spark your imagination:

Kitchen: Art Center, Housekeeping Play Area, Water Table, Science Lab, Office Space, Indoor Garden, Puzzles and Games (store these in a cupboard, on a low pantry shelf, or on a drop-down shelf installed underneath the kitchen table), Play-Alone Space (tack or tape a sheet to the edge of the table to make a "tent"; roll it up and secure with clothespins when not in use).

Bedroom: Nap Corner, Large-Motor Area (for those who don't mind a few "monkeys jumpin' on the bed"; place an old mattress on the floor to protect from falls), Age-Specialized Play Space (for school-age children only, or infants and toddlers only), Cozy Corner, Book Space, TV Area (keeps TV out of general-access areas).

Living Room: Cuddle, Reading, or Music Area (on upholstered furniture), Dramatic Play or Puppet Area (for an inexpensive puppet theater, use a curtain with a square cut in it, hung on a spring rod in a doorway), Puzzle or Block Play (store blocks on large trays or in shallow drawers that slide under the couch when not in use), Large Muscle Area.

Bathroom: Water Play, Messy Art Area, Sand (or rice or bean) Table (cover with a piece of plywood when not in use; a covered cushion stapled to the top with a skirt added to cover table legs converts a low sand table to a pretty ottoman).

Dining Room: Puzzle, Game, Art Area (store materials nearby in buffet or shelves that you can conceal with pretty curtains), Dramatic Play, Science Area.

Remember that your home is yours. It doesn't have to be House Beautiful. It only has to be what *you* want; demand that it serve *your* desires.

■ Space problems are best solved by space management. If possible, avoid using the same area for more than one activity. That limits when either one can happen. Space management means everything has its own place to happen, naturally, whenever it needs to.

■ Set your own pace. If reorganizing your entire space seems overwhelming, plan one space at a time. It may take a few weeks to get everything to where you want it to be, but that's okay. Sometimes gradual change is easier for everyone, especially children.

■ Planning new activity areas does not have to be expensive. If you don't have the money to buy beanbag chairs for your new cozy corner, use some old couch cushions you've cleaned up. Arrange pillows around a no-longer-needed crib mattress. If you can't afford a playhouse for the children's dramatic play area, find a sturdy appliance box. You'll find many other inexpensive ideas at the end of this chapter, gathered from caregivers who used their creativity instead of spending money or doing without necessities.

One caregiver repaired a garage-sale changing table; it now serves as a changing surface and infant cubbyhole for diapering supplies.

Hang on to these thoughts and your optimism as you begin this final process toward your ideal child care home.

Choosing How to Improve Your Space

There are two ways to plan for change. You can use the checklist in this section to identify and work on problem areas one at a time, or you can follow the step-by-step process given in the next section, which approaches your home as an entire unit. If you only have a few difficulties, or if you don't have the time or energy to start from scratch to design your space, the checklist may be right for you. If you have space problems coming out your ears and the whole house is driving you crazy, think about using the step-by-step plan. Read through them both to see which one appeals to you.

A Checklist for Shortcuts to Change

This section lists each of the activity areas we have discussed. For each area, there are two lists for you to check off problems. The use problem list contains three major potential problems: storage, access, and traffic. The quality problem list contains the attributes of space discussed in Chapter 4: light, sound, ventilation, temperature, and openness (accessibility was discussed as an attribute of space also, but it is put in the first list because it is so likely to be a problem).

For each area, decide if storage, access, or traffic are problems. If so, place a check mark by them. These problems are likely to be the most difficult to solve and the ones that need the most attention. If you have any activity areas that don't show those problems but still don't work as well as you'd like them to, read through the second list and check off where light, sound, ventilation, temperature, and openness are problems. Use the line to the right of each item for notes.

Note: If you have more than one of a certain area (for example, you may have two or more privacy areas), note which area has the problem.

Once you have pinpointed your trouble spots, work on them one at a time, keeping in mind what you have learned in the earlier chapters. Be sure that you don't solve one problem by causing another in a different area. For example, don't devote a kitchen cupboard to art supplies if it means you will be short on storage for utensils.

Indoor Child Care Activity Areas

Transition/Entry

- ☐ Storage _____
- ☐ Access _____
- ☐ Traffic _____

- ☐ Light _____
- ☐ Sound _____
- ☐ Ventilation _____
- ☐ Temperature _____
- ☐ Openness _____

Meals

- ☐ Storage _____
- ☐ Access _____
- ☐ Traffic _____

- ☐ Light _____
- ☐ Sound _____
- ☐ Ventilation _____
- ☐ Temperature _____
- ☐ Openness _____

Rest

- ☐ Storage _____
- ☐ Access _____
- ☐ Traffic _____

- ☐ Light _____
- ☐ Sound _____
- ☐ Ventilation _____
- ☐ Temperature _____
- ☐ Openness _____

Toileting

- ☐ Storage _____
- ☐ Access _____
- ☐ Traffic _____

- ☐ Light _____
- ☐ Sound _____
- ☐ Ventilation _____
- ☐ Temperature _____
- ☐ Openness _____

Cuddling

- ☐ Storage _____
- ☐ Access _____
- ☐ Traffic _____

- ☐ Light _____
- ☐ Sound _____
- ☐ Ventilation _____
- ☐ Temperature _____
- ☐ Openness _____

Privacy

- ☐ Storage _____
- ☐ Access _____
- ☐ Traffic _____

- ☐ Light _____
- ☐ Sound _____
- ☐ Ventilation _____
- ☐ Temperature _____
- ☐ Openness _____

Gym

- ☐ Storage _____
- ☐ Access _____
- ☐ Traffic _____

- ☐ Light _____
- ☐ Sound _____
- ☐ Ventilation _____
- ☐ Temperature _____
- ☐ Openness _____

Small Manipulatives

- ☐ Storage _____
- ☐ Access _____
- ☐ Traffic _____

- ☐ Light _____
- ☐ Sound _____
- ☐ Ventilation _____
- ☐ Temperature _____
- ☐ Openness _____

Indoor Child Care Activity Areas
(continued)

Books
- ☐ Storage _____
- ☐ Access _____
- ☐ Traffic _____

- ☐ Light _____
- ☐ Sound _____
- ☐ Ventilation _____
- ☐ Temperature _____
- ☐ Openness _____

Dramatic Play
- ☐ Storage _____
- ☐ Access _____
- ☐ Traffic _____

- ☐ Light _____
- ☐ Sound _____
- ☐ Ventilation _____
- ☐ Temperature _____
- ☐ Openness _____

Art
- ☐ Storage _____
- ☐ Access _____
- ☐ Traffic _____

- ☐ Light _____
- ☐ Sound _____
- ☐ Ventilation _____
- ☐ Temperature _____
- ☐ Openness _____

Music
- ☐ Storage _____
- ☐ Access _____
- ☐ Traffic _____

- ☐ Light _____
- ☐ Sound _____
- ☐ Ventilation _____
- ☐ Temperature _____
- ☐ Openness _____

Exploration
- ☐ Storage _____
- ☐ Access _____
- ☐ Traffic _____

- ☐ Light _____
- ☐ Sound _____
- ☐ Ventilation _____
- ☐ Temperature _____
- ☐ Openness _____

Sensory Play
- ☐ Storage _____
- ☐ Access _____
- ☐ Traffic _____

- ☐ Light _____
- ☐ Sound _____
- ☐ Ventilation _____
- ☐ Temperature _____
- ☐ Openness _____

Other
- ☐ Storage _____
- ☐ Access _____
- ☐ Traffic _____

- ☐ Light _____
- ☐ Sound _____
- ☐ Ventilation _____
- ☐ Temperature _____
- ☐ Openness _____

Outdoor Child Care Activity Areas

Meals

☐ Storage _____
☐ Access _____
☐ Traffic _____

☐ Light _____
☐ Sound _____
☐ Ventilation _____
☐ Temperature _____
☐ Openness _____

Cuddling

☐ Storage _____
☐ Access _____
☐ Traffic _____

☐ Light _____
☐ Sound _____
☐ Ventilation _____
☐ Temperature _____
☐ Openness _____

Privacy

☐ Storage _____
☐ Access _____
☐ Traffic _____

☐ Light _____
☐ Sound _____
☐ Ventilation _____
☐ Temperature _____
☐ Openness _____

Gym

☐ Storage _____
☐ Access _____
☐ Traffic _____

☐ Light _____
☐ Sound _____
☐ Ventilation _____
☐ Temperature _____
☐ Openness _____

Small Manipulatives

☐ Storage _____
☐ Access _____
☐ Traffic _____

☐ Light _____
☐ Sound _____
☐ Ventilation _____
☐ Temperature _____
☐ Openness _____

Art

☐ Storage _____
☐ Access _____
☐ Traffic _____

☐ Light _____
☐ Sound _____
☐ Ventilation _____
☐ Temperature _____
☐ Openness _____

Music

☐ Storage _____
☐ Access _____
☐ Traffic _____

☐ Light _____
☐ Sound _____
☐ Ventilation _____
☐ Temperature _____
☐ Openness _____

Exploration

☐ Storage _____
☐ Access _____
☐ Traffic _____

☐ Light _____
☐ Sound _____
☐ Ventilation _____
☐ Temperature _____
☐ Openness _____

Outdoor Child Care Activity Areas

(continued)

Sensory Play

☐ Storage _____
☐ Access _____
☐ Traffic _____

☐ Light _____
☐ Sound _____
☐ Ventilation _____
☐ Temperature _____
☐ Openness _____

Other

☐ Storage _____
☐ Access _____
☐ Traffic _____

☐ Light _____
☐ Sound _____
☐ Ventilation _____
☐ Temperature _____
☐ Openness _____

Indoor Family Activity Areas

Transition/Entry

- ☐ Storage _____
- ☐ Access _____
- ☐ Traffic _____

- ☐ Light _____
- ☐ Sound _____
- ☐ Ventilation _____
- ☐ Temperature _____
- ☐ Openness _____

Meals

- ☐ Storage _____
- ☐ Access _____
- ☐ Traffic _____

- ☐ Light _____
- ☐ Sound _____
- ☐ Ventilation _____
- ☐ Temperature _____
- ☐ Openness _____

Recreation

- ☐ Storage _____
- ☐ Access _____
- ☐ Traffic _____

- ☐ Light _____
- ☐ Sound _____
- ☐ Ventilation _____
- ☐ Temperature _____
- ☐ Openness _____

Toileting

- ☐ Storage _____
- ☐ Access _____
- ☐ Traffic _____

- ☐ Light _____
- ☐ Sound _____
- ☐ Ventilation _____
- ☐ Temperature _____
- ☐ Openness _____

Exercise

- ☐ Storage _____
- ☐ Access _____
- ☐ Traffic _____

- ☐ Light _____
- ☐ Sound _____
- ☐ Ventilation _____
- ☐ Temperature _____
- ☐ Openness _____

Sleep

- ☐ Storage _____
- ☐ Access _____
- ☐ Traffic _____

- ☐ Light _____
- ☐ Sound _____
- ☐ Ventilation _____
- ☐ Temperature _____
- ☐ Openness _____

Work

- ☐ Storage _____
- ☐ Access _____
- ☐ Traffic _____

- ☐ Light _____
- ☐ Sound _____
- ☐ Ventilation _____
- ☐ Temperature _____
- ☐ Openness _____

Other

- ☐ Storage _____
- ☐ Access _____
- ☐ Traffic _____

- ☐ Light _____
- ☐ Sound _____
- ☐ Ventilation _____
- ☐ Temperature _____
- ☐ Openness _____

Outdoor Family Activity Areas

Meals

- ☐ Storage _____
- ☐ Access _____
- ☐ Traffic _____

- ☐ Light _____
- ☐ Sound _____
- ☐ Ventilation _____
- ☐ Temperature _____
- ☐ Openness _____

Recreation

- ☐ Storage _____
- ☐ Access _____
- ☐ Traffic _____

- ☐ Light _____
- ☐ Sound _____
- ☐ Ventilation _____
- ☐ Temperature _____
- ☐ Openness _____

Exercise

- ☐ Storage _____
- ☐ Access _____
- ☐ Traffic _____

- ☐ Light _____
- ☐ Sound _____
- ☐ Ventilation _____
- ☐ Temperature _____
- ☐ Openness _____

Work

- ☐ Storage _____
- ☐ Access _____
- ☐ Traffic _____

- ☐ Light _____
- ☐ Sound _____
- ☐ Ventilation _____
- ☐ Temperature _____
- ☐ Openness _____

Other

- ☐ Storage _____
- ☐ Access _____
- ☐ Traffic _____

- ☐ Light _____
- ☐ Sound _____
- ☐ Ventilation _____
- ☐ Temperature _____
- ☐ Openness _____

Adult Business Areas

Office/Meeting

☐ Storage _____
☐ Access _____
☐ Traffic _____

☐ Light _____
☐ Sound _____
☐ Ventilation _____
☐ Temperature _____
☐ Openness _____

Entry

☐ Storage _____
☐ Access _____
☐ Traffic _____

☐ Light _____
☐ Sound _____
☐ Ventilation _____
☐ Temperature _____
☐ Openness _____

Parking

☐ Storage _____
☐ Access _____
☐ Traffic _____

☐ Light _____
☐ Sound _____
☐ Ventilation _____
☐ Temperature _____
☐ Openness _____

Special Events

☐ Storage _____
☐ Access _____
☐ Traffic _____

☐ Light _____
☐ Sound _____
☐ Ventilation _____
☐ Temperature _____
☐ Openness _____

Observation

☐ Storage _____
☐ Access _____
☐ Traffic _____

☐ Light _____
☐ Sound _____
☐ Ventilation _____
☐ Temperature _____
☐ Openness _____

Other

☐ Storage _____
☐ Access _____
☐ Traffic _____

☐ Light _____
☐ Sound _____
☐ Ventilation _____
☐ Temperature _____
☐ Openness _____

Step-By-Step: A New Plan for Your Home

Another option to plan for change is to take the plunge into the whole-house approach outlined below. Read through the six steps to get a feel for what the process is like; then begin, one step at a time.

Step 1. Gather your materials. You'll need this book, all of the notes and lists you have made, several large (at least 16" x 20") sheets of paper (graph paper is best), a yardstick and ruler (you can get away with just a ruler, but a yardstick will be easier for drawing out your plan), scissors, pencils and erasers, pen or marker, a tape measure, and a notebook or scrap paper for jotting down measurements and ideas.

Step 2. Make a floor plan of your home. In your notebook or on scrap paper, make a rough drawing of your floor plan. The plan doesn't have to be too accurate, just indicate the placement of each room. Take this rough sketch and your notebook, tape measure, and pencil and measure each room in your home. Jot down the measurements on the rough sketch. In the notebook, record the approximate position of any fixtures: doors, windows, plumbing, appliances, electrical outlets, lighting fixtures.

Use this information to draw a scale diagram of your home on the large sheets of paper. Decide on a proportion (1/2 inch = 1 foot works well) and make sure your paper is large enough to fit one floor on one sheet; if you have more than one floor, use one sheet per floor.

Using the yardstick, draw the outside edge of your home and fill in the rooms. Make sure that each room is where it belongs in relation to the rest of the house (this is the trickiest part; work in pencil so you can erase). Once you have a good floor plan, add details like the fixtures, again making sure each is exactly where it belongs. When you're finished, you'll have an accurate, scale drawing of your floor plan. With a pen or marker, trace over the lines to show that these borders and fixtures are permanent. Later, you can use a pencil to sketch in changes or experiment with design.

I like to use a black marker for walls and another color to indicate extras like windows, doors, and fixtures. Using different colors makes it easier for me to know at a glance what the room is like. Also, if I have erased a floor plan once too often, I will transfer it onto a clean sheet of paper, using carbon paper or by tracing, before I go over it with a marker. It's a nice extra to mount this floor plan on a piece of poster board to make it sturdier so that you will be able to use it again.

This floor plan is the canvas on which you will create your work of art: the best child care home design for you. Since some of your activity areas will be outside, make another map for any outdoor spaces. Add outbuildings, driveways, and other outdoor features. Use a smaller scale to plot your outdoor plan, depending on the size of your lot.

Step 3. Use your floor plan to experiment with activity areas and figure out which arrangement works best for you. Use the list of activity areas like those at the end of Chapters 2 and 3 to label the area forms found in Appendix 1. Cut out your area forms and trim them to the size that you want. Be generous; if you need to cut the area down a little, you can always do it later.

Some activity areas will require storage; for example, in a dramatic play area you will need storage for dress-up clothes and other props. Put an asterisk on the area forms that represent activities needing storage, so that as you arrange them on your floor plan you will instantly know whether you will need a little storage space nearby.

Step 4. Now it's time to play! For each floor plan, outdoor and indoor, make a pile of your area forms for each activity area and place them on the diagrams (see pages 105–106). Experiment with different combinations. Put all the areas that need quiet towards the center of the house, for example, and the noisier ones at the outer edge. Group the family outdoor activities in one area and the child care ones in another. Try out all of the activities needing storage along wall space, with the activities that don't require much storage in the middle of rooms.

Play! Toss your area forms in the air and see where they land. Use your sense of the silly! Put all your activities in one room and pretend you are selectively kicking them out of that room into another place. Brainstorm! Put every activity in a place it has never been. Create a whirlpool plan where activities for younger children revolve around you, but those for older ones are farther away. Put adult activities on the periphery. Let go of preconceptions and throw caution to the wind. Use your creativity; remember that you can't be creative and overly careful at the same time.

The more time you spend on this step, frivolous as it may feel, the better your ultimate plan will be. Spend a few days, using twenty minutes or so each day, on this step. As you play with your plan, jot down ideas or combinations of space that appeal to you. These ideas will be a gold mine for your final plan.

Step 5. Wasn't Step 4 fun? You made discoveries as you played, experimented, and brainstormed. Now use the notes you took in Step 4 to get serious about planning. Place each activity area in the space that seems best to you. Keep referring back to your notes to make sure you haven't forgotten any of your good ideas.

When each area, outdoor and in, has a spot on your plan, turn into a critic. Ask yourself several questions: What's not going to work? Does each space have the right kind of light, noise level, ventilation, temperature, openness, and accessibility (attributes of space from Chapter 4)? If not, can I change things so they will? Are all of my activity areas present and accounted for? What additional storage will I need to accommodate these areas? (Most caregivers find they need additional storage for something!) How about traffic? Will it flow easily or cause problems?

In *Caring Spaces, Learning Places*, Jim Greenman makes the important point that your traffic patterns affect the way children move through the space. Straight, direct pathways encourage running; meandering pathways or ones with angles encourage walking. They also encourage children to look at what is around them, to "graze" in the various activity zones you design.

Arrange and rearrange the area forms until you are happy with the answers to those critical questions above. Allow a week or more of twenty-plus minutes a day to bring your plan to a state of perfection.

Step 6. It's time to put your plan in motion by re-arranging your space. List any materials you will need to make or buy. As materials for each activity area are ready, change your space. Some providers change their space all at once in a marathon weekend; others change one area at a time. You may have only a few changes to make that won't require much time. Whatever your approach, make sure family and children are aware of the changes ahead of time. That will make the transition to the new space easier for them.

Odds and Ends

Dual-use areas are spaces that you use for home and business. By planning storage carefully, you can get a lot of mileage out of those areas. Bookshelves on casters are a time-honored tool in the provider's bag of tricks. By day, use a set of shelves supplied with toys as a room divider, to define a children's activity area. In the evening, turn them around and place them against a wall to serve as a buffet, desk, or sewing table.

If you need to convert space back and forth from business to family use, arrange your room so the conversions are quick and easy and are done at the beginning and end of the day, or less often than that. Some providers only rearrange when they are entertaining or at certain times of the year; for example, when they have a Christmas tree up in the living room.

Ask family members and the children you care for to participate in the conversions at the beginning and end of the day. That way, they will understand the two roles of your home and you. When you interview prospective clients, show them the way your home will look during the day when their child will be present, if it's not obvious during the interview.

Dividing Space

Without a doubt, you are planning for more activities, and activity areas, than your house was designed for. To keep activity areas from interfering with each other, most caregivers use room dividers. Room dividers are anything that keeps the activity areas separate. Of course, the basic room divider is a wall. But a divider can be as simple as a visual mark, such as a painted or taped line on a floor, or a change in surface, such as carpet to tile. Room dividers can be complex and serve several functions, such as the bookshelves that also serve as storage. Room dividers work to define activity areas as well as contain the activity. Some activity areas work best if they are bordered on three sides by dividers, some need only one or two. To decide how contained an activity area needs to be, think about the level of noise and action involved, and how accessible you want the space to be.

A rule of thumb for height of room dividers used with children is that they should be high enough to block other views when the child is seated inside, and low enough to see over when the child stands.

Some good options for dividing space are to use furniture, shelving, or folding screens (add wide bases for stability). Hang window shades, foamcore (a light rigid board available from art framing or art supply stores), curtains, or shower curtains from the ceiling to divide space. The advantage to these is that you can easily move them aside. If the entry to your child care home is through the kitchen, hide the door from the eating area by hanging a shower curtain or other screen. The screen provides a natural place to display notices, information, and children's artwork for the parents to see as they enter. It also gives a modicum of privacy to those who may be eating at the kitchen table.

Author Jim Greenman suggests using slotted wooden bases to support plywood or plexiglass sheets as dividers. I suggest trying that approach with heavy cardboard, too. Let the children decorate the screen, and replace it when it gets ragged. Stability is important; make dividers in L- or T-shapes or attach a divider to the back of a toy bench or box. Greenman also suggests raised or lowered surfaces for dividing, such as risers covered with carpet, lofts, platforms, pits, or corrals. If you try this, make sure they are moveable—you might not always want a platform in your living room. Raised or lowered surfaces can be effective without a large outlay of cash. Use a small wading pool lined with cushions for your cuddle or reading areas. You can inexpensively build a low loft, adding another activity area below (be sure to fence the upper area). One provider I visited added a slide to her loft.

Of course, safety is another reason to use dividers. Baby gates, half-doors, and doors with windows allow you and children to see each other while you keep small children out of unsafe areas. One caregiver, who had her laundry in the furnace room of the house, used a baby gate to keep the children in the playroom next door both safe and happy when she threw an occasional load of laundry into the washer or dryer.

Storage and Other Helpful Ideas

In addition to doing more in your home than it was probably designed for, you are undoubtedly storing more. Here are some ideas from the creative caregivers I visited while researching this book, as well as a few I developed in my child care home.

▓ Try to store everything near where it will be used. Store items for children at child-height, for example in low cupboards. Store dangerous items at least five feet off the floor.

This well-planned closet stores infant/toddler toys low, school-age toys on upper shelves, and cleaning fluids out of reach on top shelf. Note hook-and-eye lock.

▓ Use a fold-down or fold-up table near the bathroom sink for diaper changing (be sure it is padded, stable, and has a safety strap).

▓ Store diapering supplies and ointments on a shelf above the changing table for handy availability.

▓ Use an extra changing table's compartments for diaper cubbies: one for each child.

▓ Mount a roll of paper towels inside a cupboard door under your sink for hand drying by the children.

▓ Store a low stool under the bathroom sink so children can use it to reach the toilet or sink; that way, it won't be in your way at night.

▓ Pump-type plastic soap dispensers help keep sink area tidy.

▓ Use pretty baskets, hatboxes, or wooden boxes you decorate to store extra mittens and hats, or clean towels for swimming, near your entry. Hang them on the wall to keep them handy without clutter.

▓ In front of your door, install an iron grate over a hole cut into your porch. This did wonders to keep mud from getting tracked into my house.

▓ Child-height hooks are a must for coats and backpacks; leave eighteen to twenty-four inches between each one. To keep your entry area organized, hang shelves above the hooks to store additional items. Above the shelf, place a bulletin board to inform parents of things you want them to know. I used to keep a cracker jar on the shelf; when a child was ready to go home, he got to pick out a cracker. This motivated him to get ready without stalling or whining.

An attractive wicker basket provides handy storage for extra mittens and hats and adds appeal to the transition area.

▓ Store toys not in use in a place where they are easy for you to get to, but out of sight of the children. (You should always have enough toys so that you are rotating them and giving the children a change from time to time.)

▓ Place a strip of plywood a few inches high across the inside of a closet doorway, on the floor; this creates an instant toy box.

▓ Use recycled materials for storage. Clean coffee cans with tape over the rims make excellent containers for craft supplies and small manipulatives. Larger cans, taped together on their sides in a pyramid (use duct tape), create a cubbyhole system for storing naptime items such as stuffed toys or receiving blankets.

- Mount an egg carton (with holes in the egg cups) to store toothbrushes and small scissors; an upside-down supermarket strawberry basket (the plastic kind) also works well.

- A collapsing tunnel was my best investment for gym play. It served a multitude of roles and stored flat in four inches of space.

- Store dramatic play props according to theme in boxes; ask parents for additions to the boxes when you create a new theme (such as, office, store, pizza parlor, hospital, camping).

- A large draped tablecloth over a small card or side table makes a fun tent during the day; at night, store toy boxes under it.

- The space beneath cribs is ideal for storing boxed supplies; it can also be a fun hideout.

- Create an office in a closet. A plywood shelf at desk height is your work surface; use shelving above for supplies, resources, and records. Fit a chair or stool beneath the desk, along with a small wastebasket. One provider I visited had installed a computer in a closet office like this.

- Keep a lost-and-found box or basket near your transition area to toss unfamiliar possessions into until they are claimed.

- The top of your refrigerator is a handy place to store child care-only foods; use small shelves or a box or laundry basket.

- Have a hook for your coat or sweater in the transition area for quick trips outside during drop-off and pickup times.

- Mount a two-by-four along the wall two feet under coat hooks and drill in holes to accommodate dowels at a sharp angle out from the wall. Turn boots upside down and store on these dowels to dry quickly. A shoe rack will serve the same purpose; make sure it's out of the traffic pattern, though.

- Don't file your training certificates, license, and other credentials in your office area. Display them proudly on the wall in your transition area to show your professionalism to your client families. One provider I visited also displayed testimonial letters from other families in this way—a great marketing tool when potential clients visit.

- Store formula preparation materials and bottles together in a handy basket for quick preparation.

- Outdoors, a storage shed is perfect for storing riding toys, out-of-season items, and other toys; it can double as a play space when the toys are in use in the yard.

- For super-quick pickup, cover the playroom floor with a blanket, toss in all the toys, slide the blanket under the dining room table, and cover the table with a full-skirt tablecloth. You're ready to entertain.

- Sturdy cardboard boxes are great inexpensive toy boxes; let the children paint them for added visual appeal.

- A pocket on the side of an armchair or couch stores your "Story of the Day"; if it's wide, you'll be able to slide the book in (open to the page you're on) when the doorbell rings, phone rings, or baby cries.

- Use hooks and pegs to store dramatic play props so that children can see them without sifting through a large box. A changing table with compartments works well, too.

- A large sheet with elasticized corners makes an inexpensive sandbox cover children can remove and replace themselves.

- Plastic crates, tubs, and jars make wonderful storage items for crafts materials. Use the lids so you can stack the containers.

- Shallow trays are great for storing puzzles; they stack well and each puzzle has its own work surface when in use.

- Use the back of a bookshelf or sofa as a flannelboard display; staple the flannel to the flat surface; store flannel shapes right on the flannelboard or in a pocket next to it.

- Cover sturdy boxes with contact paper to make large blocks; store them flat on a large piece of cardboard with a shallow rim; slide under the bed for storage.

- A flat heavy piece of cardboard makes a good surface for block play, too, especially if the alternative is a bumpy, uneven carpet.

- Sew your own "slipcover house" to pop over a card table for an instant playhouse. Add details like windows, doors, flowers with sewing trim, or let children decorate!

- Lawn lounge chair cushions slipped inside "envelopes" you sew out of sheets make inexpensive, comfy nap mats. (Buy cushions at the end of the season for greatest economy.) Pierce sheet "envelopes" (around the cushions) to add shower curtain rings at one end; use them to hook mats onto hangers and store them in a closet.

- Display photos of children in care near the entry; update them periodically so parents get a sense of what the day is like for their child. Keep old photos in a special album to show prospective clients. They will imagine their child among the happy faces. They will also realize your attachment to the children you care for.

- If you buy or make crafted wooden toys, like rocking horses or riding toys, let them be a part of your decor; they won't need to be out of sight when company comes.

- Slip a small table and chair under a counter or table with a few coloring supplies for the shy child who would rather be with you than play in the next room while you prepare lunch.

- Sturdy decorative quilts can do double-duty as tenting material (over chairs or tables) during the day; toss on the sofa to add a homey touch at night.

- Use a hammock or a plastic wading pool for storing stuffed animals.

- Sturdy laundry baskets make great toy storage. When empty, they are also fun for children to play in.

- In closets, store items for youngest children on lowest shelves, increasing age with height. On the topmost shelf, store items you don't want children to get out themselves.

- Keep young infants in a carrier on your back as you prepare meals, clean up, or set up projects for the other children.

- Use a large keg or drum to store balls outdoors; empty and turn on its side for hideout fun.

- A low window garden in the kitchen doubles as a science/nature interest area. Store plant care items in pretty flowerpots nearby.

- Keep medicines on a kitchen shelf or cupboard, not in the bathroom. It's less likely children will get into them unobserved in the kitchen.

- If you have a nook in your kitchen, slip a rocking horse in there to entertain a restless youngster who isn't behaving with the other children. You'll be able to keep an eye on her while you prepare or clean up meals.

- Use bureaus, files, and storage boxes made of cardboard; they are an inexpensive storage option that will last if cared for (and if out of reach of the children).

- A handheld vacuum mounted near the table or counter provides easier clean up.

■ Keep at least a few toys within reach in the kitchen. Books and puzzles at the table will keep children occupied for a few minutes while you finish fixing lunch. Store the books with your cookbooks to keep them handy.

■ Always have a special place for library books so they don't get mixed up with your books; it's easy to forget which ones belong to you. The same is true for books the children bring from home.

■ Strategically placed mirrors can help you see from one area into another for those times you'd like to be in two places at once.

■ Have a game library in a cupboard or closet; only one can be checked out at a time. Before borrowing another one, the game must be returned with all its pieces. This works for puzzles and crafts, too.

■ Store a few attractive toys among your books and music in areas like the living room. Those toys can add a little touch of humor and children will know they are a part of what happens in that space.

■ The logical place for children's tapes, both audio and video, is near tape players they can learn to operate themselves.

■ A chalkboard in the kitchen lets children draw while you cook; use it to draw a menu to let them know what's for lunch, too.

■ Do you have only one coat closet in your transition area and no room for hooks? Add hooks and shallow cubbies to the inside of your coat closet door for the children; family coats can be hung on the clothes rod.

■ If you use a gate in your play yard, hang it high enough to clear a few inches of snow, so it doesn't get frozen open (or closed). Hang it low enough to keep children from crawling out.

■ A garage wall is a great storage surface; hang garden tools high, children's playthings low. Install hooks to hang car seats, strollers, and buckets of toys to keep them handy but out of the way.

■ Paint a stripe on your garage floor to remind children where bikes are to be stored. You can even paint parking spaces; one for each bike or wagon.

■ Use a microwave stand as a storage area for booster seats, bibs, and other mealtime necessities.

■ Live in a second-floor apartment? Use the wall along the stair as your parent information and art display space.

▥ Use side rails on twin beds to make safe sleeping space for toddlers. For a child who is just starting to sleep in a twin bed without rails, slide the bed next to the wall and raise the outer bed legs slightly with wooden shims or blocks; the child will not roll off onto the floor.

▥ For a baby or child with chest congestion, raise the head of the bed or crib with blocks under the bed legs. Coughing is less likely to interrupt sleep.

▥ Use an awning or tent over a sandbox to keep sun from burning children or making sand too hot.

▥ Use shallow wire baskets or shelving suspended on the shower curtain rod to hold water play toys over the bathtub.

For more ideas, visit other caregivers in your area. A half-day spent touring other child care homes can provide a wealth of exciting, innovative ideas; and you'll know that the ideas were designed by people who are coping with the same situations you face. Some child care resource agencies offer tours of child care homes periodically; if yours does, take advantage of seeing how others plan activity areas.

You're All Set!

In this book, you've learned a great deal about your family, your business, and the space that both occupy. If you have let the needs of family and business be the foundation for their activities and the space used for them, your child care home will run more smoothly. You should find yourself with a little more time to devote to the things you feel are most important.

A Quick Review

The process of change started with thinking about space in terms of the people the space serves. We looked at the needs of each person in your business and family constellations, then at the activities which satisfy those needs. We thought about space and what makes it pleasant and workable for the activities that happen in it. Chapter 5 brought all of those concerns together in a process that used creativity to solve space dilemmas.

You are now in a position to understand more about space planning than most, if not all, of the people you are living and working with. That means that some of those people might have a hard time understanding the reasons for the changes you are making. They may not see how important it is for everyone to cooperate with the changes. Your task will be to educate them. This will be easy if you have involved all of them in your planning process, so that the changes are not a surprise. But you may still have some explaining to do. You will have the greatest chance of success in getting people to accept change if you can show them how they will benefit from it, whether directly or indirectly.

Reworking the Plan

As you begin to use your newly designed space, you might find that not everything works as well as you had hoped. You may realize yourself, or others may make you aware, that a certain activity area or combination of areas has inherent problems. If you face this situation, try to find out if the problem is a transitional one, caused simply by the difficulty of adjusting to a change. If that is the case, ask the people involved to try it out for a short time and see if they can adjust. If you still hear complaints, take them seriously and head back to the drawing board. That doesn't mean you have to redo the whole plan, just find a way to adjust it so that the concerns will be met. Your family or business associates may have useful suggestions that can help you make the necessary changes.

Looking Ahead

Designing space around people means that the space has to work in a multi-dimensional way, including the fourth dimension, time. But we know that people, their needs, and activities, change over time. You can count on needing to change your space from time to time to accommodate that. As your family grows or shrinks, as you age, as children in care mature, or as older children leave and younger ones enroll, the space may need to change. Plan to review this process from time to time, especially when you know changes are imminent. Once you have completed this process for the first time, you will have gained the skills to do it more quickly and easily the next time around.

A Final Note

Being a professional in child care and taking a professional approach to solving problems has brought you to read this book and try the process of change suggested in it. If that has been a helpful experience, expand your library of child care resource books. Many references that can help you resolve issues you face as a provider are available—and each book has its own perspectives. (Some of these references are listed in the Bibliography section.) Reading about how other caregivers face their problems, and about new trends and solutions as they become known, is an exciting and useful way to keep abreast of your profession. If you're going to have a career in child care, you might as well take advantage of the resources that can help you do the best job you can. Good luck.

Planning Tools

Use these area forms to plan where each of your activity areas should go on your floor plan. Each area is divided by shape and color; use the rectangular ones for child care activities and the oval ones for family activities. Customize your areas further by using the clear forms for daytime activities and the shaded ones for those that happen in the evening or at night.

Label each area form (which you can photocopy, cut out, trace, or copy) with one of the activity areas you will need. The forms are made of concentric shapes so you can decide how large the activity area needs to be. The area forms are designed with a 1/2 inch = 1 floor plan in mind, but reduce their size if your floor plan is drawn to a smaller scale.

Vendor Resources

The vendors listed below will help you plan for and acquire the equipment you need for a child care home. In addition to catalogs, however, ask your local resource agency, child care food program, or other support agency if they have a toy lending library that will let you try out new equipment before you invest in it.

Most of the companies listed here will be happy to send you a catalog, either free of charge or for a small charge applicable to your first purchase. When ordering a catalog, specify that you want the institutional version; some companies put out a general or home version that may not have everything you are interested in. When ordering an item from a catalog, mention that you are operating a child care facility and ask the vendor if they offer a discount. Sometimes resource agencies or child care home networks can order in bulk and receive discounts.

Each of these vendors carries a large cross-section of merchandise including children's furniture, room dividers and storage items, indoor and outdoor toys and learning supplies, and arts and crafts supplies.

Childcraft
20 Kilmer Road
Edison, New Jersey 08818-3081
800-631-6100

Chime Time
934 Anderson Drive
Homer, NY 13077
800-423-5437

Constructive Playthings
1227 East 119th Street
Grandview, MO 64030-1117
800-255-6124

Educational Teaching Aids
199 Carpenter Avenue
Wheeling, IL 60090
800-445-5985

Environments, Incorporated
P.O. Box 1348
Beaufort Industrial Park
Beaufort, SC 29901-1348
800-342-4453

J. L. Hammett Company
Early Learning Division
P.O. Box 9057
Braintree, MA 02184
800-225-5467

Judy/Instructo
4325 Hiawatha Avenue South
Minneapolis, MN 55406
800-526-9907

Kaplan School Supply Corporation
P.O. Box 609
Lewisville, NC 27023-0609
800-334-2014

Lakeshore Curriculum Materials Company
2695 Dominguez Street
P.O. Box 6261
Carson, CA 90749
800-421-5354

Nasco
901 Janesville Avenue
Fort Atkinson, WI 53538-0901
or
Nasco West
1524 Princeton Avenue
Modesto, CA 95352-3837
800-558-9595

Primary Educator
1200 Keystone Avenue
P.O. Box 24155
Lansing, MI 48909-1773
800-444-1773

This list does not constitute an endorsement of these companies or their products.

Bibliography

Bredekamp, Sue, ed. *Developmentally Appropriate Practice in Early Childhood Programs Serving Children from Birth through Age 8*. Washington, D.C.: National Association for the Education of Young Children, 1986.

Carlsson-Paige, N., and D. E. Levin. *Who's Calling the Shots? How to Respond Effectively to Children's Fascination with War Play and War Toys*. Philadelphia, Pennsylvania: New Society Publishers, 1990.

Greenman, Jim. *Caring Spaces, Learning Places: Children's Environments That Work*. Redmond, Washington: Exchange Press, 1988.

Harms, Thelma, and Debby Cryer. *Space to Play and Learn*. Chapel Hill: University of North Carolina, 1985.

Harms, Thelma, and Richard Clifford. *The Family Day Care Rating Scale*. New York: Teachers College Press, Columbia University, 1989.

Kritchevsky, Sybil, and Elizabeth Prescott. *Planning Environments for Young Children: Physical Space*. Washington, D.C.: National Association for the Education of Young Children, 1969.

Modigliani, Kathy. "Assessing the Quality of Family Child Care: A Comparison of Five Instruments" (1990).

Rice, Judith. *Those Mean Nasty Dirty Downright Disgusting but. . .INVISIBLE Germs*. St. Paul, Minnesota: Redleaf Press, 1989.

Other Redleaf Press Publications

Basic Guide to Family Child Care Record Keeping : Fourth Edition— Clear instructions on keeping necessary family day care business records.

Business Receipt Book — Receipts specifically for family child care payments improve your record keeping; 50 sets per book.

Busy Fingers, Growing Minds — Over 200 original and traditional finger plays, with enriching activities for all parts of a curriculum.

Calendar-Keeper — Activities, family day care record keeping, recipes and more. Updated annually. Most popular publication in the field.

Child Care Resource & Referral Counselors & Trainers Manual — Both a ready reference for the busy phone counselor and a training guide for resource and referral agencies.

Developing Roots & Wings: A Trainer's Guide to Affirming Culture In Early Childhood Programs — The training guide for Root & Wings, with 11 complete sessions and over 170 training activities.

The Dynamic Infant — Combines an overview of child development with innovative movement and sensory experiences for infants and toddlers.

Enrolllment/Medical Form — Information required by most states, from health history to emergency parental consent.

Family Child Care Contracts and Policies — Samples contracts and policies, and how - to information on using them effectively to improve tour business.

Family Child Care Tax Workbook — Updated every year, latest step-by-step information on forms, depreciation, etc.

Heart to Heart Caregiving: A Sourcebook of Family Day Care Activities, Projects and Practical Provider Support — Excellent ideas and guidance written by an experienced provider.

Kids Encyclopedia of Things to Make and Do — Nearly 2,000 art and craft projects for children aged 4-10.

The (No Leftovers!) Child Care Cookbook — Over 80 child-tested recipes and 20 menus suitable for family child care providers and center programs. CACFP creditable.

Parent/Provider Policies — Easy-to-use, 2-part carbonless form that helps you create a thorough, professional parent agreement.

Pathways to Play — Help children improve their play skills with a skill checklist and planned activities.

Practical Solutions to Practically Every Problem: The Early Childhood Teacher's Manual — Over 300 proven developmentally appropriate solutions for all kinds of classroom problems.

Roots & Wings: Affirming Culture in Early Childhood Programs — A new approach to multicultural education that helps shape positive attitudes toward cultural differences.

Sharing in the Caring — Packet to help establish good relationships between providers and parents with agreement forms and other information.

Snail Trails and Tadpole Tails — A fun nature curriculum with five easy-to-do, hands on units that explore the life-cycle of these intriguing creatures: snails, worms, frogs, praying mantises and worms.

Those Mean Nasty Dirty Downright Disgusting but... Invisible Germs — A delightful story that reinforces for children the benefits of frequent hand washing.

CALL FOR CATALOG OR ORDERING INFORMATION 1-800-423-8309